THE
PRIVATE SOLDIER
UNDER
WASHINGTON

THE
PRIVATE SOLDIER
UNDER
WASHINGTON

by

CHARLES KNOWLES BOLTON

new introduction
by
Steven C. Eames, PhD

Illustrated

**CORNER HOUSE
HISTORICAL PUBLICATIONS**
Gansevoort, New York   12831
1997

Originally reprinted in hard cover by Corner House in
1976

Revised edition (soft cover) reprinted by:

Corner House Historical Publications
14 Catherine Street: PO Box 207
Gansevoort, NY   12831

Most recent soft cover printing indicated by the number
below:

10 9   8   7   6   5   4   3   2   1

ISBN   0-87928-012-3   Hard Cover, 1976 edition
ISBN   0-87928-117-0   Soft Cover, 1997 edition

The Corner House Historical Publications edition is an
unabridged reprint of the original edition published in
September 1902 by Charles Scribners & Sons, New York.
This edition includes a new introduction by Steven C. Eames,
PhD.   Printed on acid free paper in the United States of
America.

TO MY WIFE

Ethel Stanwood Bolton

CONTENTS

ILLUSTRATIONS

Illustrations

Illustrations

INTRODUCTION

In closing his book, *The Private Soldier under Washington*, Charles Knowles Bolton summed up his efforts. "Whether France or Washington or the patriot army contributed most to bring about the peace of Paris in 1783 is of little moment. France and Washington long ago had their due; it has been the purpose of these pages to give the private soldier under Washington whatever share in the victory was his by right of danger, privation, and toil that he endured." Although published in 1902, and colored by its own era, Bolton's effort remains an excellent, if not the best, introduction to the common American soldier in the War for Independence.

The late nineteenth century was a period known as the Colonial Revival. The centennial of the Declaration of Independence in 1876 had awakened a tremendous feeling of nostalgia for Americans. Faced with the aftermath of a war that had almost destroyed the country, and numerous political scandals in Washington D.C., Americans in 1876 hearkened back to a Golden Age, to a time when the country was one in its quest for liberty, and men like George Washington, Thomas Jefferson and Benjamin Franklin founded this great nation. This Colonial Revival manifested itself in many ways, from the creation of patriotic organizations and historical societies to architecture. It also produced new histories and biographies. George Washington, Franklin and Alexander Hamilton all received new treatments, and many poems and popular novels emerged in the press or from publishing houses.

Bolton's life presents a classic example of the Colonial Revival. Born on November 14, 1867, he was the son of Sarah Knowles Bolton, a published poet and writer of novels. His mother achieved some notice of her work, but no lasting fame. Charles followed his mother's lead at first. His first two books were novels, *On the Wooing of Martha Pitkin* (1894) and *The Love Story of Ursula Wolcott* (1895). But soon after, the Colonial Revival fever would strike. Charles Bolton was instrumental in forming the historical society in his hometown of Brookline, Massachusetts. From all accounts he was driven to this, and became the real fire behind the organization. In 1897 he published *Brookline, The History of a Favored Town*. Bolton's employment placed him in an excellent position to do research. While he was serving as the Town Librarian, he founded the Brookline Historical Society. Then shortly before the turn of the century he became the librarian for the Boston Athenaeum, a position he held for the rest of his life. As a librarian Bolton's opportunities for research and interests varied, as his numerous publications reveal. He published an *American Library History* in 1911, and five years before his death in 1950 he published *Our American Language*. He even retained his mother's influence and published another novel in 1912. But history remained the primary focus of his research and writing. Bolton's history books included *Scotch-Irish Pioneers* (1910), *The Founders* (3 volumes, 1919-1926), and *The Real Founders of New England* (1929).

However, the work best remembered today is *The Private Soldier under Washington*. Among the numerous books being written about the Revolution in his time, all the biographies of Washington, Franklin, Hamilton, etc., Charles Knowles Bolton noticed a gap, or perhaps more accurately, an unintentional disregard for the common soldier of the Revolution. He did not dispute Washington's greatness, indeed his respect for the nation's founding father is quite evident. Bolton only wished to remember and understand the soldiers who suffered and sacrificed; who endured, that Washington might have an army to lead to victory. Although these sentiments seem out of place in our modern, cynical world, social historians and students of the American Revolution generally applaud this first effort to rescue the common soldier from obscurity.

Charles Knowles Bolton wrote when the historian's craft was in transition. Historians were taking on the mantle of science and professionalism, yet many still made their presentation to the general public. These historians based their analysis on documentation and the evaluation of sources, but their prose was purely narrative. Perhaps Francis Parkman, although writing earlier than Bolton, is the best known of this genre. Another example is Alice Morse Earle, a prolific writer of colonial history and a contemporary of Bolton. Parkman and Earle based their work on primary sources, yet employed a somewhat romantic but completely accessible prose style. Bolton fits this transitional mold. His writing was sentimental at times. In describing the march of the army on the Sullivan campaign against the Iroquois, Bolton wrote, "The way through the Indian country was often picturesque and strange, leading over high, barren mountains from which the wide plains, like another world, could be seen below, then down into wooded ravines, dark and damp with vapor." He could also allow his imagination to take over, as when he described a soldier writing in his journal, "with brows puckered to concentrate his thoughts and keep from his mind a babel of voices." However, Bolton based his analysis on primary documents such as letters, journals and government orders and papers. He also questioned his sources, evaluating the motivation of the authors. "One must keep in mind," he wrote, "the fact that nearly all contemporary authorities were influenced by the bitter spirit of the times."

Bolton's structure can be disconcerting at first. The first two chapters provide an overview of the War for Independence and the problems in raising and maintaining an army. What follows are chapters dealing with the common soldier, including "Material Needs," "Firelock and Powder", "Officer and Private", "Camp Duties", "Camp Diversions", etc. However, even under these specific titles, Bolton can stray. He seemed to let the sources lead him on his journey, so there is very little attempt at chronology, and the transition between topics can be abrupt, even startling. Yet what an amazing number of topics. The reader should approach this work like a smorgàsbord, where we can forgive the lack of order because the variety is so wonderful.

Bolton covers clothing, weapons, camp life, music, religion, celebrations, amusements, punishments, hospitals, prison - the list seems endless. He discusses the effects of weather, problems with supply, housing, and training. He describes everything from the building of huts to the procurement and preparation of food in great detail, and throughout the book he quotes soldiers' letters and journals extensively. Although Bolton wrote during the Colonial Revival, he did not gloss over or ignore the ugly images left behind. He was willing to reveal that American soldiers could break the rules, steal, destroy, and even be sadistic. He could boldly proclaim that "Yankee Doodle" probably was not played or sung that much. His only reluctance concerned sex, his single comment on the subject being, "Sensuality is not often mentioned in the diaries or letters of the soldiers, although references are not wanting." Considering the number of quotes he uses, the modern reader is left wondering about those tantalizing references. Whether this is a comment on Bolton's day or our own, I leave for others to judge.

Indeed, in addition to his reticence to discuss sex, those interested in Bolton's time will glean some interesting comments from this work. The late nineteenth century brought change to America, including urbanization, immigration, industrialization, changes that disturbed many Americans, including Charles Bolton. He laments the passing of craftsmen, the cordwainer, the cooper, broom maker, itinerant weaver and miller. "Who of us, looking through the advertising pages of a popular magazine, will feel any sentiment for the factories and mills pictured there - those unlovely successors of the vine-covered shops of the cordwainer, the cooper, the gunsmith?" Unfortunately, his comment about "red men" and his understanding of the black contributions to the war also place Bolton in his time period.

Bolton does make mistakes, usually when he strays from his sources and attempts generalizations. He claims the American soldiers carried a "trusty flintlock made usually by the hand of a village gunsmith". He is carried away by sentiment there, and did not understand that the manufacture of firearms was beyond the capabilities of village gunsmiths, who usually restricted themselves to repair. At the start of the War for Independence most Americans carried weapons of foreign manufacture and import, and, despite some efforts at large scale production, would continue to rely on French contributions and captured British weapons to arm their soldiers. At another point he describes Americans as "a pioneer people...accustomed to danger, and...familiar with firearms", and yet a few pages later he described the Philadelphia militia as "unaccustomed to hardship". The latter involved a cited primary source, the former the Colonial Revival mindset.

Since the 1960's historians using the techniques and approaches of the "New Social History" have studied the common soldier of the American Revolution in depth, particularly who they were, why they fought, and what they experienced. These historians have taken Bolton to task for insisting that the Continental soldiers were stalwart freemen and tradesmen. Scholars understand now the impact of the three year enlistment and how it drove the land-owning freemen away from military service. However, while modern historians discount some of Bolton's conclusions, they recognize the continued value of his work, because none of these modern histories have covered such a broad sweep of topics, and none of them wrote for such an inclusive audience as Bolton.

If I may be permitted, I would like to propose an analogy, which may seem a bit bizarre to the reader, but is somehow appropriate. Cookies and whole milk are not as good for you as leafy vegetables and whole bran, and in fact nutritionists will claim that cookies and whole milk contain elements harmful to you. And in this age of high tech, glossy-packaged and overly-promoted foods, cookies and whole milk seem quaint and old-fashioned. But as a snack, cookies and whole milk are very good and very satisfying. Bolton's work is not perfect. He made mistakes, he generalized, he exhibits the prejudices of his time. His florid prose is often quaint and old-fashioned. The use of modern social science techniques and computers has produced some remarkably in-depth studies of the common soldier over the last few decades that improves upon Bolton's research relating to some specific issues. One would expect, that with time, research methods and accessibility to additional resources should improve, thereby enhancing the viability of our work. Even modern historians agree that Bolton's work is still based on solid research and evidence, and as an introduction and overview of the American army in the War for Independence, Charles Knowles Bolton's *The Private Soldier under Washington* remains very accessible, very good and very satisfying.

Dr. Steven C. Eames
Mount Ida College, 1997

Steven C. Eames is a professor of history at Mt. Ida College in Newton, Massachusetts. He received his PhD in American History at the University of New Hampshire in 1989. His interest in military history has made him a life long living history enthusiast. In Civil War living history, he has progressed to the command of the recreated Civil War 28th Massachusetts Regiment and also serves as a field officer with the Irish Volunteers. Dr. Eames has written many articles on the common soldier in American history and is currently working on a Civil War history of Nahant, Massachusetts.

PREFACE

MUCH has been written about the American Revolution, but our knowledge of the private soldiers of the patriot army is confined chiefly to Washington's description of their sufferings at Valley Forge. Their story is to be found in a line here and there scattered through the mass of contemporary literature. In sifting this material, it has seemed best to give in every case the name of the authority who saw what he described. No student, however, would willingly forget the labors of those later writers who have done so much to make easier the way for others.

I record with pleasure my obligation to Professor Edward Channing, of Harvard College, for very many valuable suggestions; and also to Mr. Albert Matthews, whose knowledge of the language and customs of the period has been of great service to me.

C. K. B.

Pound Hill, Shirley,
Massachusetts, July, 1902.

The Private Soldier Under Washington

I

The Origin of the Army

WHEN the colonists in America rose in rebellion against the English Government in 1775, they occupied scarcely more territory than had been won from the wilderness a century earlier. Pioneers from the shores of the North Sea had crossed the Atlantic to make for themselves homes; the more venturesome had forced their way to the head-waters of the coast rivers to build block-houses for trade and defence. Little by little they and their descendants cut away the timber along the banks of many pleasant streams and planted grain. And now, at the southward, their lands reached from the ocean to the Appalachian range—the watershed of the Potomac, the James, the Roanoke, the Santee, the Savannah and the Altamaha rivers. Farther north they cleared and tilled the country which is drained by the Susquehanna, the Hudson, the Connecticut, the Kennebec, and the Penobscot.

Here was a theatre of war with great possibilities for the strategist who knew the topography thoroughly, and could marshal the rivers and hills like forces in reserve to checkmate his antagonist. Throughout Washington's campaigns near New York the Hudson River on the east and the Delaware on the west served to keep the British in check. The manœuvres of Gates and Greene in the Carolinas were everywhere influenced by the broad streams that cross the country. But rivers were dangerous allies, and when made part of a great plan might, by the fortunes of war, prove ruinous to an army. In the campaign of 1777 Burgoyne was to gain control of the Hudson in order to separate the men of New England from their brothers in rebellion; but he accepted a position within the bend of the river at Saratoga and was compelled to surrender. In the expedition of Cornwallis in 1781 the converging streams of the York and the James, which were to protect his army, held him like a trap as soon as the French allies came into possession of the sea.

The political divisions show that England laid claim to the eastern part of America, with the exception of Florida. Massachusetts still included the territory between the western part of Nova Scotia, now called New Brunswick, and

[4]

New Hampshire, later known as Maine; and the land between the Connecticut River and Lake Champlain, afterward the State of Vermont, was at this time within the bounds of New York. The rich country between the upper Mississippi and its tributary the Ohio had but recently been added to the Government of Quebec. There were few English inhabitants in this region, and the French stockades and trading villages, such as Detroit, Vincennes on the Wabash, and Kaskaskia, were important only as settlements along the water highway from Canada and the Great Lakes to New Orleans. The southern English colonies already looked westward to the Mississippi for their expansion.

Beyond all this region lay the untouched forests which gathered rains for the far-reaching waters of the Rio Grande, the Colorado, the Arkansas, and the Missouri—the possessions of Spain.

The English colonies in 1775 had a population of two and a half million people, less than a third the number then in Great Britain and Ireland. Moreover, above half a million of these people were negroes, barred very generally from military service; many others refused from their religious views to bear arms; and a considerable

[5]

minority of the citizens—more than a third of the men of influence, said Adams—opposed an appeal to force. It was fortunate for America that the war began in New England, which had few Tories and slaves, and was able, by furnishing a large part of the patriot army, to show a strong front to the enemy.

Earlier in the century there had been little to draw together the various races then settled upon the continent, isolated as they were by religious differences, social distinctions, and the imperfect means of travel. But a steady policy of irritation and repression on the part of the English Government quickened the sympathies of the people, and led to the perfection of intercommunication and to the dissemination of political ideas. The arbitrary restriction of trade and abrogation of privileges by an unseen power 3,000 miles away aroused the colonies to a sense of their common danger.

The presence of an English garrison at Boston, and the enforcement of acts designed by Parliament to crush out the revolutionary spirit in Massachusetts, made the colony a centre of the coming storm. The members of a convention of delegates from the towns and districts in Suffolk County, meeting in September, 1774, declared in

[6]

language vigorous, if a little florid, that to arrest the hand about to ransack their pockets, to disarm the parricide who stood with a dagger at their bosoms, and to resist the usurpation of unconstitutional power, would roll their reputation upon a "torrent of panegyric" to the abyss of eternity.[1] With their future fame secured, they set about frankly to prepare for the conflict, calling upon the people to elect their militia officers, and acquaint themselves with the art of war, that King George might not make an easy prey of "a numerous, brave, and hardy people."[2] The action taken by several of the towns about Boston was if possible more marked. Brookline, for example, appointed a committee in September to examine into the state of the town as to its military preparation for war "in case of a suden attack from our enemies."[3]

On October 26, 1774, the Provincial Congress, sitting at Cambridge, chose a committee of safety with power to collect military stores, and, if necessary, to summon and support the militia. With the delegation of this authority to a specific

[1] Journals of each Provincial Congress of Massachusetts (Lincoln), pp. 601, 602.

[2] *Ibid.*, pp. 603, 604.

[3] Muddy River Records, p. 248.

[7]

body of leaders, the opposition to Great Britain ceased to be wholly legislative, for the committee had the necessary power to maintain armed rebellion. The military measures of this period, proposed in convention and carried by vote, in time of peace and within three or four miles of the British garrison, were a test of New England courage and determination that deserve recognition.

At the same time a plan of organization for the militia was outlined. Field officers were ordered to enlist, if possible, a quarter of the total number of militiamen for emergency service under the direction of the committee of safety; these companies were to consist of at least fifty minute-men each, and were to elect their own company officers.[1] Twenty years earlier, alarm-list companies had been organized to repel the Indians; they may be considered as survivals of the regiments that were in King Philip's time ordered to be ready to march at a moment's warning; and these in turn can be traced to the companies

[1] Journals Provincial Congress of Massachusetts, p. 33. The Continental Congress recommended to the Colonies, July 18, 1775, to form similar companies of minute-men. The term minute-men appears September 21, 1774, in the Journal of the Worcester County Convention. (Journals Provincial Congress, pp. 643, 644.)

of thirty men from each hundred of the militia which in 1645 were to be prepared " at halfe an howers warning." Thus had the training in arms and in preparation against surprise and attack been handed down from the days of Myles Standish and Simon Willard.[1] The committee on the state of the province drew up, December 10, 1774, an address to the people which urged the towns and districts to pay their local militia for their services, in order to encourage them " to obtain the skill of complete soldiers."

These preparations were well known in Boston, and Lord Percy, who was for a time in command of the British troops there, referred often to them in letters to his father; as early as September 12th he said that the rebels " did not make a despicable appearance as soldiers."[2] He knew that training-day had ceased to be a perfunctory ceremony.

The Provincial Congress resolved, on April 8, 1775, that an army should be raised and established, and other New England colonies should be asked to furnish their quotas of men for the general defence. The records of the committees of safety and supplies show that various stores

[1] Green's Groton during the Revolution, p. 3.
[2] Percy to his father, September 12, 1774; MS. at Alnwick.

were being collected at this time, such as spades, pick-axes and bill-hooks, iron pots and wooden mess-bowls, carpenters' tools, cartridge - paper, powder and fuses, grape and round shot, bombs, mortars, musket-balls and flints, molasses, salt fish, raisins, oatmeal, and flour.[1]   From the 8th of March to the 14th of April, 1775, sundry persons under the direction of John Goddard were carting through the quiet country roads that lead to Concord casks of balls, barrels of linen, hogsheads of flints, loads of beef and rice, quantities of canteens and other articles.[2]

To seize these stores, so specifically enumerated in the old thong-bound account-book of wagon-master Goddard, Lieutenant - Colonel Francis Smith,[3] with the flank companies of the Tenth Regiment of foot and of several other corps, embarked from Boston Common at about half-past ten o'clock Tuesday night, the 18th of April,[4] crossed the Charles River, and began the march

[1] Journals Provincial Congress of Massachusetts, p. 505 *et seq.* Records Committee of Safety.

[2] Goddard's Account Book ; MS. in Brookline Public Library.   Reprinted in part in Brookline Historical Publication Society, Publication No. 15.

[3] Cannon's Historical Record of the Tenth Regiment, p. 36.

[4] Gage's account in Journals Provincial Congress of Massachusetts (Lincoln), p. 679.

which was to bring on the American Revolution. He met and dispersed the forewarned minute-men on Lexington Green at five o'clock of the morning of the 19th of April; he marched on to Concord, destroyed the stores, and commenced the return; at half-past two his men, thoroughly exhausted from their rapid march back toward Lexington, lay down within the hollow square formed by reënforcements which Lord Percy had led out from Boston.

The retreat of the regulars along the country road has often been pictured in words; the redcoats were harassed by the farmers who (to use Percy's own phrase) surrounded and followed them like a moving circle,[1] firing from trees and stone walls. A British soldier, apparently in " Chatham's division of marines," had his hat shot off his head three times, lost his bayonet by a ball, and had two holes in his coat,[2] as he pushed on to Charlestown. Colonel Smith's men from the Tenth Regiment wore at this period three-cornered cocked hats bound with white lace; scarlet coats faced and turned up with bright yel-

[1] Percy to General Harvey, April 20, 1775; MS. at Alnwick.

[2] Journals Provincial Congress of Massachusetts (Lincoln), p. 683.

[11]

low, and ornamented with white lace; scarlet
waistcoats and breeches; white linen gaiters reaching above the knee; white cravats, and buff
belts.[1] They were brave men of many battle-
fields, and their discomfiture was a sight to stir
the blood of every man in homespun who reached
the scene. Each town has its story of that mus-
ter-morning, of the minute-man who left his
plough in the furrow, the bucket at the well-
sweep, or the fodder at the door of the cattle-
shed. In some towns not above half a dozen
able-bodied men remained at home through the
19th of April, and the killed, wounded, or missing
were credited to twenty-three different towns and
villages.[2]

The British reached Bunker Hill, across the
narrow neck which joins Charlestown to the main-
land, as the dusk began to make visible the flash
of the muskets. Their pursuers halted while the
militia officers held a consultation at the foot of
Prospect Hill; a guard was formed, sentinels
were posted as far as the approach to the Neck,
and patrols were sent out to watch the enemy.
The militia then withdrew to Cambridge. Another guard went to the Brookline and Roxbury

---

[1] R. Cannon's Historical Record, p. 35.
[2] Journals Provincial Congress of Massachusetts, p. 678.

shores, south of Boston, to cover that territory until morning. On the 20th Cambridge was searched for beef, pork, and cooking utensils, while Roxbury furnished a good supply of ship-bread for the hungry men. Before noon the committee of supplies in Concord had sent word that they were using every effort to forward provisions. Thus were the first difficulties overcome, and an armed force began the siege of Boston.[1]

The men who encamped about Boston had fought with perseverance and resolution;[2] they were not raw recruits, for many had contended in the wars with French and Indians, and their names may still be seen on the King's muster-rolls.[3] They were not a rabble recruited from the low ranks from which a city mob is drawn. College and professional men did their part. The death of a justice of the peace, who was a graduate of Harvard and held his commission under the Crown, caused a heated discussion in the British press; some said that he was a spectator, for they could not believe that the movement was respectable in the character of its supporters.[4] General

[1] Heath's Memoirs (1798), pp. 14–16.
[2] Lord Percy's letter, *supra.*
[3] Massachusetts Archives, Colonial and Revolutionary Rolls.
[4] Gazetteer and New Daily Advertiser, July 4, 1775.

Howe, writing to Lord Dartmouth a few months later, stated half the truth when he said that the Continental army contained many European soldiers and most of the young men of spirit in the country, who gave diligent attention to the military profession.[1]   Lord Percy had held that the Americans were " a set of sly, artful, hypocritical rascals, cruel, and cowards,"[2] but after the battle of Lexington he declared that the rebels showed an enthusiasm and a courage to meet death that promised an insurrection not so despicable as was imagined in England.   Percy was quick to see that the Indian method of fighting from behind trees and stone walls was proof not of cowardice, but of ability to profit by conditions; and, said he, " they know very well what they are about."[3]

Soon after the events of the 19th, men in the companies encamped near Boston were asked by the committee of safety to enlist for service until the end of the year, or for a shorter period at the committee's discretion.[4]   A vigor-

[1] Howe's letter, January 16, 1776, quoted in Washington's Writings (Ford), vol. 3, p. 353.

[2] Lord Percy to H. Reveley, August 8, 1774 ; MS. at Alnwick.

[3] Lord Percy to Harvey, April 20, 1775.

[4] For the oath see Journals Provincial Congress of Massachusetts (Lincoln), p. 201.

[14]

ous circular letter, dated April 20th, was sent to the neighboring towns urging the enlistment of an army to defend wives and children " from the butchering hands of an inhuman soldiery "; and on the 21st the committee decided to raise an army of 8,000 effective men out of the Massachusetts forces.[1] In the meantime the Provincial Congress had been hastily summoned, and had resolved, April 23, 1775, to raise 13,600 men. Proposals were also made " to the congress of New Hampshire, and governments of Rhode Island and Connecticut colonies " for furnishing men in the same proportion, as an army of 30,000 was deemed necessary. A month later 24,500 men had been collected in the several colonies.

So thoroughly had the work of organization gone on in the colonies during 1773, 1774, and the spring of 1775, that an appeal for men when the siege of Boston began was immediately successful. Throughout the country a network of local committees, controlling militia compa-

---

[1] Records Committee of Safety. Journals Provincial Congress (Lincoln), pp. 518–523. Each company was to have a captain, lieutenant, ensign, four sergeants, a fifer, drummer and fifty men ; nine companies to form a regiment. The men were promised good officers.

nies and post-riders, bound together the opposition to the King; this network was like a fuse which ran over thousands of miles of wood, meadow, and farm-land. The people had been able to follow every movement of the hostile British Parliament through the aid of the committees of correspondence and inquiry. These committees, formed in each colony at the suggestion of the Virginia House of Burgesses in March, 1773,[1] watched the approaching storm, tested the loyalty of those who professed to welcome it, and guided the popular indignation.

When the battle of Lexington came, the colonies were as well prepared for war as the poor dependencies of a powerful nation could be. The first news of the battle was brought to the ears of Putnam at Pomfret the next day, and to Arnold at New Haven a day later;[2] John Stark in New Hampshire heard it in good time. At ten o'clock on Wednesday morning, the 19th, Palmer, of the Massachusetts committee of safety, wrote a letter from Watertown to alarm the country "quite to Connecticut," entrusting it to a rider who was to ask for fresh horses as he went. At Fairfield, Connecticut, this message was overtaken by one

---

[1] Calendar of Virginia State Papers, vol. 8.
[2] Stiles's Diary, vol. 1, p. 540; Durfee's Fitch (1843), p. 8.

This Day, about Noon, arrived a second EXPRESS from New-England, with the following important Advices.

Wallingford, Monday, April 24, 1775.

DEAR SIR,

COLONEL WADSWORTH was over in this place, most of yesterday, and has ordered 20 men out of each company in his regiment, some of which had already set off, and others go this morning. He brings accounts which came to him authenticated from Thursday in the afternoon. The King's troops being reinforced, a second time, and joined, as I suppose, from what I can learn, by the party who were intercepted by Col. Gardner, were then encamped on Winter Hill, and were surrounded by 20,000 of our men, who were entrenching. — Colonel Gardner's ambush proved fatal to Lord Percy, and another General Officer, who were killed on the spot, the first fire — To counterbalance this good news, the story is, that our first man in command, (who he is I know not) is also killed — It seems they have lost many men on both sides — Colonel Wadsworth had the account — a letter from Hartford. — The country beyond here are all gone, and we expect it will be impossible to procure horses for our waggons, as they have, and will, in every place employ, themselves, all their horses — In this place they send an horse for every 6th man, and are pressing them for that purpose — I know of no way but you must immediately send a couple of stout able horses, who may overtake us at Hartford possibly; where we must return Mrs. Noyes's, and Meloy's, if he holds out so far — Remember the horses must be had at any rate — I am in the greatest haste, your entire friend and humble servant.

JAMES LOCKWOOD.

N. B. Col. Gardner took 9 prisoners, and is clubbed their firelocks and came over to our party, Col. Gardner's party consisted

of 700, and the regulars 1800, instead of 1200 as we heard before; they have sent a vessel up Mystick River as far as Temple's Farm, which is about half a mile from Winter Hill. These accounts being true, all the King's forces, except 4 or 500, must be incamped on Winter Hill.

At the instance of the gentlemen of Fairfield, just departed from hence, this is copied verbatim from the original, to be forwarded to that town.
Isaac Beers,
Pierpont Edwards.

New-Haven, April 24.
half past 9 Forenoon.

The above copy, came authenticated, from the several towns through which it passed, by the following gentlemen, viz.

Fairfield, 24th April, 3 o'clock afternoon, Thaddeus Burr, Andrew Rowland, Elijah Abel.

Norwalk 24th April, 7 o'clock afternoon, John Cannon, Thaddeus Betts, Samuel Gramao, committee.

Stamford, 24th April, 13 o'clock evening, John Hait jun. Samuel Helton, David Webb, Daniel Gray, Jonathan Waring, jun.

Greenwich, April 25, 3 o'clock morning, Amos Mead.

The above gentlemen write, that in each town, they shall hold themselves in readiness to match more men immediately, if wanted, and request their brethren in the Western towns and governments to do the same, and that all material intelligence, shall be forwarded with speed.

Some accounts mention, that the soldiery had been guilty of some shocking barbarities, in wantonly burning houses and murdering old men, women and children, but of these, we shall not mention particulars, till the arrival of more certain and circumstantial accounts.

Printed from the attested Original, by JOHN HOLT.

How the news was carried. An express from New England.
(From the Gerard Bancker collection of broadsides.)

written at three o'clock Thursday morning, and attested by the committee of correspondence from town to town. The news reached **New York** on Sunday, the 23d, at noon, and confirmed the rumors that had already begun to circulate; by four o'clock a messenger was on his way to Philadelphia. About two o'clock of the 25th a second express from New England reached New York, his papers having been attested at New Haven, Fairfield, Norwalk, Stamford, and Greenwich. The same evening a copy reached Elizabethtown; at ten it was in Woodbridge and signed; at midnight it had reached New Brunswick across the Raritan and half way through New Jersey; three hours and a half brought the good horse and its rider to Princeton; at half-past six they were in Trenton, and by seven the attested papers were on their way to Philadelphia. The committee of the city sent the news at midday to Chester; at nine the man drew up at Newcastle, having followed the Delaware through the gathering darkness; he reached Christeen Bridge at midnight with orders to forward the papers day and night; at half-past four, in the gray of the morning of April 27th, he was at the Head of Elk in Maryland, and after travelling seventeen hours, touching Charlestown on the way, he reached Baltimore at ten that night. A hard ride along the tortuous shore of Chesapeake Bay through the entire night brought the news to Annapolis, where Carroll of Carrollton, Tilghman, and other patriots attested the papers and spread the tidings.

Still on, through Alexandria and Dumfries, a long Sunday journey brought the papers to Fredericksburg, where the committee signed at half-past four. Carter Braxton met the messenger at King William on May 1st, nearly a fortnight after the battle. To the southward went the news, through Surry County, Williamsburg, Smithfield (May 3d), Nansemond, Chowan in North Carolina, Edenton, Beaufort County, Bath, Newbern (May 6th), to Onslow County, where the committee received it at ten o'clock Sunday morning of the 7th. At Wilmington on Cape Fear River, Harnett, of the committee, wrote, " For God's sake send the man on without the least delay," and so the news was borne to the committees of Little River and Georgetown, and on to Charleston in South Carolina.

What a ride and for what a cause! Through rain and sun and starlight this firebrand of rebellion was carried. This was a ride that made the colonies into a nation, and the nameless messengers and their horses deserve a page in history.[1]

The Continental Congress resolved on June 14th that six companies of expert riflemen be immediately raised in Pennsylvania, two in Maryland, and two in Virginia to reënforce the army near Boston; each company was to consist of a captain, three lieutenants, four sergeants, four corporals, a drummer or trumpeter, and sixty-eight privates.[2] The besieging army was temporarily under the command of General Artemas Ward who received his commission from Massachusetts as commander-in-chief on May 20th. Four days earlier, however, the Provincial Congress had sent Dr. Church to Philadelphia to offer the direction of the army to the Continental Congress. On June 15th George Washington was appointed "to command all the Continental forces"; on July 4, 1775, it was announced in general orders that the "troops of the United Provinces of North America" were taken over by Congress. The army then numbered not more than 14,500 men,[3]

[1] American Archives IV., vol. 2, col. 363; and in North Carolina Colonial Records, vol. 9, p. 1229.

[2] June 22d two more companies were ordered to be raised in Pennsylvania.

[3] Washington to Congress, July 9, 1775. Journals Provincial Congress of Massachusetts, p. 482.

including perhaps the newly organized train of artillery which had been authorized in April by the province.[1]   There existed also a coastguard which had been raised to defend the sea-board towns upon which the British made depredations in their excursions after food.[2]

The army had scarcely settled down to besiege Boston before the presence of slaves and free negroes gave rise to the question of their status in the army.   They had not, apparently, been included in the companies of militiamen and minute-men which were organized and drilled in the winter of 1774–75; but the moment a call for men went out, the black men presented themselves for service.   In May the committee of safety faced the matter frankly in a resolve which is ethically curious for its differentiation of principles when applied to freemen and to slaves. This resolve read :

" That it is the opinion of this committee, as the contest now between Great Britain and the colonies respects

[1] Journals Provincial Congress of Massachusetts, p. 220, and Journals Continental Congress, July 29, 1775.

[2] These men were to furnish good firelocks and were to receive powder from the towns in which they were stationed, the powder to be paid for by the colony.   They were to serve through December, 1775, and to receive $36 a month and subsistence. —Journals, pp. 402, 412, 426.

Orders

By his Excellency

George Washington Esquire,

Commander in Chief

of the forces

of the

United States

of America.

Head Quarters, Cambridge, July 3rd 1775

Parole, Lookout.   Counter Sign, Sharp.

The Colonels Commanding Officer of each Reg. are ordered forthwith, to make two Returns of the number of men in their respective Regiments, distinguishing such as are sick, wounded absent, on furlough. And also the quantity of ammunition each Regiment now have.

It appearing by the Report of Henry Woods, the Officer of the main guard, that one William Alford is confin'd for taking two horses belonging to some Persons in Connecticut, but that he has made satisfaction to the injured parties, who request that they may not be longer detain'd as witnesses. It is ordered that he be discharged, and after receiving a severe reprimand, be turned out of camp.

Punishment of a soldier.
Page from Washington's order book, July 3, 1775.

the liberties and privileges of the latter, which the colonies are determined to maintain, that the admission of
any persons, as soldiers, into the army now raising, but
only such as are freemen, will be inconsistent with the
principles that are to be supported, and reflect dishonour
on this colony ; and that no slaves be admitted into this
army upon any consideration whatever." [1]

The Provincial Congress considered the matter,
and laid it on the table. Free negroes continued
to serve in the American camp, and were conspic-
uous at the battle of Bunker Hill in June;
one man, Salem Poor, "behaved like an experienced officer as well as an excellent soldier,"
according to the testimony of Colonel Prescott.[2]
They were obedient soldiers and useful labor-
ers, of a less mutinous spirit than some of their
white brothers.[3] In July the Provincial Congress barred out all negroes, but the question
came to the front again in the autumn of 1775,
when the reënlistment of troops for 1776 was
under discussion; the council of general officers

[1] Moore's Historical Notes on the Employment of Negroes in
the American Army, p. 5. Committee of Safety, May 20,
1775. American Archives IV., vol. 2, col. 762.

[2] Massachusetts Archives, vol. 180, p. 241. Quoted also
by George Livermore.

[3] General Thomas to John Adams. Massachusetts Historical
Society Proceedings, 1862–63, p. 186.

voted October 23d to reject slaves and free negroes.[1]

Lord Dunmore's proclamation in November, 1775, freeing all indented servants and slaves who were able and willing to bear arms, to induce them to join the British army, probably forced a general order issued by Washington, December 30th, allowing continental recruiting officers to enlist free negroes, and promising to bring the whole matter to the attention of Congress. Finally, as a compromise, Congress permitted those who had served faithfully at Cambridge to reënlist.[2] Blacks continued to serve in the army despite all legislative efforts to exclude them; a return of negroes in Washington's command August 24, 1778, shows that seven brigades then had an average of fifty-four in each.[3] A Hessian officer said in 1777: "One sees no regiment in which there are not negroes in abundance, and among them are able-bodied, sturdy fellows."[4] The employment of negroes met with approval in many of the colonies, but not in the extreme South. Rhode Island purchased the freedom of

[1] Washington's Writings (Ford), vol. 3, p. 162.
[2] Journals of Congress, January 16, 1776.
[3] Moore's Historical Notes, p. 17 *et seq.*
[4] Schloezer's Briefwechsel, vol. 4, p. 365.

[22]

slaves before enrolling them as soldiers, trusting to Congress for financial aid, and many men in Colonel Christopher Greene's regiment were obtained in this way.[1] The South, true to its traditions, refused the urgent appeals of Colonel John Laurens in 1779 and in 1782 for permission to enlist colored troops, although Congress had at last come to favor the scheme, and it was backed by Alexander Hamilton and General Greene.[2] Southern statesmen were by no means of one way of thinking on the slavery question and on the employment of negroes as soldiers. The views which Laurens expressed to his father, while highly creditable to a young man reared in South Carolina, were not such as would appeal to most slave-holders. He wrote: " I would advance those who are unjustly deprived of the rights of mankind to a state which would be a proper gradation between abject slavery and perfect liberty. . . ." And again: " I am tempted to believe that this trampled people have so much human left in them, as to be capable of aspiring to the rights of men by noble exertions, if some friend to mankind would point the road, and give them a pros-

[1] Governor Greene's letter, June 3, 1779; in R. I. Historical Society Collections, vol. 6, pp. 235–236.

[2] Washington's Writings (Ford), vol. 10, p. 48.

The Private Soldier Under Washington

pect of success. . . . Habits of subordination, patience under fatigues, sufferings and privations of every kind, are soldierly qualifications, which these men possess in an eminent degree." Laurens said with truth that five thousand black soldiers might change the course of the next campaign. But it was the institution of slavery, not the character of the slaves, as Washington himself intimated, that placed obstacles in the way.[1] Madison was disposed to favor the use of blacks in regiments with white officers and a fair proportion of white soldiers. His correspondent, Joseph Jones, could see the blessings of emancipation, but he wanted no hasty measures and nothing so uncertain in its results as the drafting in of slaves. His statement of the case is strong and reasonable:

"If they [the enemy] once see us disposed to arm the blacks for the field, they will follow the example and not disdain to fight us in our own way, and this would bring on the southern States inevitable ruin. At least it would draw off immediately such a number of the best labourers for the culture of the earth as to ruin individuals, distress the State, and perhaps the Continent,

[1] Army Correspondence of Colonel John Laurens, pp. 108, 115–118.

[24]

when all that can be raised by their assistance is but barely sufficient to keep us jogging along with the great expence of the war."[1]

The private who marched in his company to reënforce the army about Boston felt somewhat as a voter did at a parish or a town meeting. The company to which he belonged was his, and the officers owed their authority in part to his favoring vote. A private from New Jersey has described the mode of procedure : the men were "sworn to be true and faithful soldiers in the Continental army, under the direction of the Right Honorable Congress. After this we chose our officers. . . . When on parade, our 1st lieut. came and told us he would be glad if we would excuse him from going, which we refused; but on consideration we concluded it was better to consent; after which he said he would go; but we said, ' You shall not command us, for he whose mind can change in an hour is not fit to command in the field where liberty is contended for.' In the evening we chose a private in his place."[2] Could there be a more vivid pict-

[1] Jones to Madison, quoted in Madison's Writings (Hunt), vol. 1, p. 106.

[2] Aaron Wright's Revolutionary Journal; in Historical Magazine, July, 1862, p. 209.

ure of the private soldier at this period of the war? There is the respect (kept well in hand) that is due the chief legislative body known as the "Right Honorable Congress"; there is also evidence of a matter-of-fact management of officers which must have been unknown to the benighted British soldier; then comes that word of philosophy so characteristic of the age and of the undisciplined volunteer; and finally in the election of a private as first lieutenant is shown that disregard of station which gives the picture its last touch.[1]

On July 19, 1775, the army exceeded 17,000 men, including Gridley's regiment and Crane's company of artillery;[2] in the latter part of 1775 Washington had about 19,000 effective men

[1] The oath referred to above was no doubt as follows (Journals of Congress, June 14, 1775) :—

I . . . have, this day, voluntarily enlisted myself, as a soldier, in the American continental army, for one year, unless sooner discharged : and I do bind myself to conform, in all instances, to such rules and regulations, as are, or shall be, established for the government of the said army.

Privates who took the oath were to find their own arms and clothes, and were to receive $6⅔ or 40 shillings a month. — Journals of Congress, June 14, 1775. For the Massachusetts oath see Journals Provincial Congress, May 8, 1775.

[2] Washington's Writings (Sparks), vol. 3, p. 488.

near Boston, most of whom would return home when their terms of enlistment expired in December or at the end of the year.[1] To pay off this army on the old establishment, as it was called, and to provide one month's pay in advance for the new establishment which was to be enlisted to carry on the siege, required £278,-228 15s. or the sum of $927,429½.[2] In the new army, which was to have 20,372 men including officers,[3] the soldiers (except drummers and fifers) were to furnish good arms or when provided by Congress to allow a deduction of six shillings from their pay; a stoppage of ten shillings a month was to be made from each man's pay until his debt for clothing was cancelled.[4] Although this was an unsatisfactory method at times, and the payment of wages by the calendar month was even more disliked,[5] the soldier was told to be cheerful over the fact that he received higher pay than private soldiers ever had in any

[1] American Historical Review, vol. 1, p. 292 ; Washington's Writings (Sparks), vol. 3, p. 493.

[2] Washington's Writings (Ford), vol. 3, p. 296.

[3] Journals of Congress, Nov. 4, 1775.

[4] Washington's Orderly Book, October 31, November 12, 1775, in his Writings (Ford), vol. 3, pp. 191, 221.

[5] Rev. B. Boardman's Diary ; in Massachusetts Historical Society Proceedings, May, 1892, p. 412.

former war.[1]   Another blessing of war came
when the colonies, at the request of Congress,
prohibited the arrest of Continental soldiers for
debts under thirty-five dollars, or the attachment
of their property for sums under one hundred
and fifty dollars.[2]

When the principles involved in the creation of
a new army for the year 1776 came under consideration, the duration of the contest was very
uncertain.   Congress recommended to Massachusetts and Connecticut a two-year or a one-year
term ; it was found that men hesitated to pledge
their services for the entire war, and at that time
the military profession was so little known and so
untried by those who were fitted only for the
ranks that they did not turn to it as readily as
they did to farming.   John Adams contended
that a regiment might possibly be obtained in
New England " of the meanest, idlest, most intemperate and worthless, but no more.   A regiment was no army to defend this country.   We
must have tradesmen's sons and farmers' sons, or
we should be without defence, and such men
certainly would not enlist during the war, or for

[1] Washington's Orderly Book, October 31, November 12,
1775, in his Writings (Ford), vol. 3, pp. 191, 221.
[2] Journals of Congress, December 26, 1775.

long periods, as yet. The service was too new; they had not yet become attached to it by habit. Was it credible that men who could get at home better living, more comfortable lodgings, more than double the wages, in safety, not exposed to the sicknesses of the camp, would bind themselves during the war? I knew it to be impossible."[1] This is the view of a shrewd observer of New England character, a politician who, it may fairly be said, knew those of whom he wrote. On the other hand, he does not seem to count the influence of patriotism and love of adventure; these certainly would have moved some to forsake their comforts and good wages for the army, even had the term of service been long. With a small permanent force many troubles of the next few years might have been banished, provided, of course, the force was large enough to carry on the war. The size of the army that could have been raised will always remain debatable.

The advantage of long over short terms of enlistment has the weight of all authorities familiar with raising, equipping, and drilling recruits. Washington himself said on this subject: " The

[1] John Adams's Autobiography, in his Works (C. F. Adams), 1851, vol. 3, p. 48.

evils arising from short or even any limited in-
listment of the troops are greater and more extensively hurtful than any person (not an eye-
witness to them) can form any idea of. It takes
you two or three months to bring new men in
any tolerable degree acquainted with their duty;
it takes a longer time to bring a people of the
temper and genius of these into such a subor-
dinate way of thinking as is necessary for a soldier. Before this is accomplished, the time approaches for their dismissal, and you are beginning to make interest with them for their con-
tinuance for another limited period; in the doing
of which you are obliged to relax in your discipline, in order as it were to curry favor with them,
by which means the latter part of your time is
employed in undoing what the first was accom-
plishing. . . . Congress had better determine
to give a bounty of 20, 30, or even 40 Dollars
to every man who will Inlist for the whole time."[1]
Joseph Hawley, of the Provincial Congress, might
be quoted in reply that no bounty would induce

[1] Washington to Reed, February 1, 1776, in his Writings
(Ford), vol. 3, p. 400. For some suggestive remarks on
short enlistments and an untrained militia during the wars sub-
sequent to the Revolution, see Hazard Stevens's address, October
14, 1898, " Reform the militia system " (Boston, 1898).

WE whose Names are under written, do hereby severally Inlist ourselves into the Service of the United American Colonies, and severally promise, and engage to continue in such Service, until the first Day of December. 1776: unless sooner Discharged; and to furnish ourselves each with a good effective Fire Arm, and if possible, a Bayonet fitted thereto, a Cartridge Box and Blanket, or in Lieu of a Bayonet. a Hatchet or Tomahawk : —We also in like Manner promise and engage to obey all the lawful Commands of the Officers appointed or to be appointed over us, pursuant to the Resolves of the General Court of the Colony of Massachusetts-Bay ; and under the Direction of such Officers to march, when ordered, with the utmost Dispatch, to the Northern Department or Canada, and to be subject to all such Rules and Regulations, in every Respect, as are provided for the Continental Army.   July   1776.

An enlistment blank of the Massachusetts Bay Colony, 1776.

WE the Subscribers do hereby severally inlist ourselves into the Service of the United American Colonies, until the first Day of January next, if the Service should require it ;—and each of us do engage to furnish and carry with us into the Service aforesaid, a good effective Fire Arm and Blanket ; (also, a good Bayonet, Cartridge Pouch, and a Hatchet, or Tomahawk, or Cutting-Sword, if possible ;) and we severally consent to be formed by such Person or Persons as the General Court shall appoint, into a Company of Ninety Men, including one Captain; two Lieutenants. one Ensign; four Serjeants, four Corporals, one Drum, and one Fife, to be elected by the Company and commissionated by the Council, and when formed, we engage to March into Canada. with the utmost Expedition, and to be under such Field Officers as the General Court have appointed, or shall appoint; and we further agree, during the Time aforesaid, to be subject to such Generals, or superior Officers, as are or-shall be appointed; and to be under such Regulations, in every Respect, as are provided for the Army aforesaid. Dated the   of A. D. 1776.

An enlistment blank of 1776.

New England men to enlist for more than two years.[1]

The popular feeling in the autumn of 1776 is well shown by the following extract from a letter of Josiah Bartlett, a delegate in Congress from Rhode Island: "I am fully sensible," he writes, "of the great difficulties we labour under by the soldiers being enlisted for such short periods, and that it would have been much better had they at first received a good bounty, and been enlisted to serve during the war. But you may recollect the many, and, to appearance, almost insuperable difficulties that then lay in our way. No money, no magazines of provisions, no military stores, no government; in short, when I look back, and consider our situation about fifteen months ago, instead of wondering that we are in no better situation than at present, I am surprised we are in so good." [2]

The colonies, particularly at the north where democracy was less tolerant of militarism, dreaded a standing army,[3] which to most minds had

---

[1] American Archives V., vol. 1, col. 404.

[2] *Ibid.*, vol. 2, col. 118.

[3] "The well disciplining the militia renders useless that dangerous power and grievous Burden, a *standing Army.*"—T. Pickering in the Essex Gazette, January 31, 1769, p. 1.

some close but mysterious connection with " enlisting for the war." Among northern officers
this feeling crystallized into a leaning toward
colony affiliation in preference to Congressional
control; Governor Ward of Rhode Island, who
was no enemy to the Continental system, attributed the slow enlistment under the new establishment to dislike of plans brought forward through
southern influence favorable to an army "wholly
Continental" or attached solely to the Congress.[1]

The difficulties which were encountered in
raising, equipping, and supporting a regular army
led to the frequent use of militia. This in turn
hindered the pursuit of agriculture and brought
about a greater scarcity of food,[2] while the constant coming and going of men, some of whom
had been hired at exorbitant rates—$150 in spe-
cie for five months of service—increased the
consumption of supplies without adding propor-
tionately to the effective force. Men were to be
seen in the country taverns and upon the roads,
some returning from service, some away on furlough, and too many away through desertion.

[1] Samuel Ward to his brother, November 21, 1775; in
W. Gammell's Life of Ward (Sparks's Library of American
Biography, second series, ix., p. 327).

[2] Washington's Writings (Ford), vol. 8, p. 395.

In a war of great successes their presence in the country might have encouraged enlistments by awaking a warlike spirit; in a war of delay and hardships they must have done little or nothing to offset the heavy cost of travel and rations while on their journey. The amusing experience of a not over-scrupulous private while on his travels has been related by himself:

" The 20th [February, 1780] I leaves Mr. Lowdens [at New Windsor] and Crosses the North River and Comes to Fishkill, and gos to a offiser to git an order to Draw provision, and he hapened to be there that I Drue provision on the Day before. he said, Did not you Draw Eight Days yesterday (I found I was Cached). I said yes but that was to Carry me to Boston. He said how I Could draw at Litchfield and at Hartford. I said I did not want to Draw it there to have to Carry it." [1]

The captains and lieutenants were kept busy training raw recruits; this work was not left to sergeants and corporals, as it seemed best to have a closer bond between the officers and their men.[2] Baron Steuben was an ardent advocate

[1] Elijah Fisher's Journal, p. 13. The punctuation has been supplied.

[2] A. Graydon's Memoirs, pp. 117–122.

[33]

of personal contact of officer and private; he had no patience with the British custom of giving over the awkward squads to sergeants. He rose at three in the morning during the manœuvres, says his biographer North, drank a cup of coffee and smoked a single pipe while his servant dressed his hair; at sunrise he was on horseback. A year or two later when his theories of training had come to have their influence he said : "Do you see there, sir, your colonel instructing that recruit? I thank God for that." [1] His own interest in the rank and file was very real. One day during the roll-call Steuben heard a private answer to the name Arnold; he summoned the man to his tent, told him that so good a soldier should not bear a traitor's name, and gave him permission to be known thereafter as Steuben.[2]

Increase in the price of food and clothing which accompanies war tends to check the enlistment of married men, and the rise in artisans' wages still further operates in the same direction where men have families dependent upon them for support. Under these conditions the bounty or pay must be advanced, as was ably set forth in the time of the Civil War by Governor Oliver P.

[1] Kapp's Steuben (1859), pp. 130, 131.
[2] *Ibid.*, p. 290.

[34]

Morton of Indiana in an address to Congress in 1862, entitled "Increase of Pay of private Soldiers." Colonel Cortlandt related to General Gates a case that tells of the married man's trials: "The bearer hereof, William Foster, a soldier in Colonel Wynkoop's regiment, having lately buried his wife, and has with him now at this place five small children, and no way to provide provision for them unless he can be discharged to go to a small farm he has some distance from here, and begs me to write in his favour to procure his discharge." [1]

The privations of army life were trifling when compared with the worry that was caused by a knowledge of the privation at home. The steady increase of taxes in 1779–82 and the departure of farm-hands to the front drove women almost to desperation. State and town officials endeavored to aid and support the wives and children of the soldiers,[2] and to check and punish those who forced up the necessities of life beyond the prices agreed upon by state or county conventions and accepted by the towns.[3] Salt, so nec-

[1] American Archives V., vol. 2, col. 573.

[2] Miss Caulkins's New London (1852), p. 503. Wheeler's History of Brunswick, Me., pp. 125, 126, 170.

[3] New London, p. 503 ; Parmenter's Pelham, Mass., p. 137.

essary to every farm that had live stock, rose from about thirty cents a bushel to almost as many dollars; tea and molasses also advanced to a price that bore hard upon the poor.[1] Women did the hard work of the farm, with a suggestion or word of advice at long intervals from their absent husbands. A private at the siege of Boston wrote to his wife and children in 1775:

"I must Bee Short! gat 2 or 3 Bushel of Solt as quick as you Can for it will Bee Deer, and what [cattle?] the Barn will Not Winter [*i.e.*, hold through the winter] the Saller Sall [cellar shall?]; and give them as good a chance [to thrive] as you Can and as for my Coming home I Can Not if you Sant ten men in my Room."[2]

There was at the same time, if Dr. Benjamin Rush is right in his assertion, an increase in the birth-rate in America, implying prosperity or at least easy circumstances among a considerable part of the population.[3] In the larger centres of trade the increased circulation of money, the growth in importation of goods and in transpor-

[1] Stevens's Facsimiles, No. 2082.
[2] Parmenter's Pelham, p. 129.
[3] Massachusetts Magazine for 1791, p. 360.

tation of grain, with an undoubted demand for labor, all combined to give an appearance of good times to that class which has nothing to lose by war. The men about the taverns, the small shops, and the wharves married and cared for their families. Dr. Rush declares that from the year 1776 to the close of the war beggars were rarely seen. The burdens of the war were not wiped out, but were placed upon the owners of the soil; poverty was lifted from the town poor to fall upon the farmers.

As it became more and more difficult for farmers to support their families, it is no surprise to find that after the first enthusiasm had died away, the enlistment of men was slow and unpleasant. An officer would go to the village tavern, wax eloquent, and pass round the toddy until some country lad was moved to sign his name to the papers; but unless an officer was shrewd, he came away with his money spent and no recruit at his back. That his errand was sometimes a relief to a town may be inferred from a note in Graydon's Memoirs:

"Mr. Heath . . . helped us . . . to a recruit, a fellow, he said, who would do to stop a bullet as well as a better man, and as he was a truly worthless dog, he held that the neighborhood would be much indebted to us for taking him away."[1]

Another writer has pictured the motley throng of men and boys, in all stages of intoxication, that gathered about a recruiting officer in a seaport town. When the band which he employed to gather a crowd had stopped playing he stood at the street corner beneath a flag and sang in a comical manner :

> All you that have bad masters,
>   And cannot get your due,
> Come, come, my brave boys,
>   And join with our ship's crew.

This was followed by cheers and a commotion in which men were persuaded or driven to the wharves and aboard a privateer that was ready for a cruise.[2]

Many undesirable army recruits were sent to camp, and upon one occasion General Parsons forwarded seven useless fellows to Hartford that the Connecticut Legislature might see what imposition was practised by some recruiting officers.[3] Congress decided in January, 1776, to

[1] Graydon's Memoirs, p. 135.
[2] E. Fox's Revolutionary Adventures, p. 56.
[3] Washington's Writings (Ford), vol. 9, p. 156.

disapprove the employment of prisoners, and thus closed to the enlistment officer a hopeful field for his efforts. When voluntary enlistments fell off the authorities resorted to drafts; these were not always successful, especially in the disaffected districts, where many officers and men so obtained proved to be Tories at heart.[1] When the militia were well fed and clothed, with good officers to make them contented, numbers of the rank and file could be trusted at times to go home to gather recruits. Colonel Thomson, of South Carolina, on one occasion wished to send most of his men away on furlough, so that they might return in time with lusty country lads at their heels.[2]

No doubt there was an element less readily moved to enlist by patriotism than by material and tangible considerations, however deep, strong, and broad the unseen current of loyalty might be. A warm, pleasant day in the autumn of 1775 and a cheering glass of grog helped the officers who were recruiting for the army of 1776.[3] This, the testimony of an officer at Roxbury, fairly repre-

[1] American Archives V., vol. 3, col. 206.

[2] Thomson to Rutledge and to Howe, June 9, 1777, in Salley's Orangeburg County, S. C., pp. 450, 451.

[3] J. Fitch, Jr.'s, Diary, November 14, 1775; in Massachusetts Historical Society Proceedings, May, 1894, p. 80.

sents the easy-going spirit which governed men of a certain class. They were not the privates who studied by the camp-fire and kept diaries, but many were none the less useful soldiers. A battle sifts men by a process unknown to the days of peace, bringing to the front unexpected heroes. Can you not see two of them now—Haines at Bemis Heights, astride the muzzle of a British brass twelve-pounder, ramming his bayonet into the thigh of a savage foe, recovering himself to parry the thrust of a second, and, quick as a tiger, dashing the same bloody bayonet through his head; recovering again, only to fall from the cannon, shot through the mouth and tongue; lying two nights on the battle-field until thirst, hunger, and loss of blood overcame him, then in the ranks of the dead made ready for burial; and from all this recovering for three years more of service and a green old age:[1] or again, that unknown dare-devil whose swaying figure stood out upon the parapet of the entrenchments about Yorktown, brandishing his spade at every ball that burred about him, finally going to his death, " damning his soul if he would dodge."[2]

[1] Kidder's First New Hampshire Regiment, p. 23.
[2] Captain James Duncan's Diary ; in Pennsylvania Archives, second series, vol. 15, p. 748.

"The common people," said General Greene, referring to New England, "are exceedingly avaricious; the genius of the people is commercial from their long intercourse with trade."[1] This spirit prompted many from the towns to make the best bargain possible when they enlisted for the year 1776, while the farmers, who usually saw very little money, coveted the bounty that was offered. Washington had an independent income; the poorer officers and the rank and file depended for their subsistence and the support of their families upon their meagre and uncertain pay. This difference in condition did not impress Washington with sufficient force in his first encounter with the army. There was no doubt "a dirty, mercenary spirit" which to some extent made possible "stock-jobbing and fertility in all low arts to obtain advantages of one kind and another," but that it "pervaded the whole" one must doubt. The diaries of officers and privates, written with no thought of publication, show a loyalty and in some instances a religious earnestness that must indicate widespread moral purpose.[2]

[1] Greene to Ward, December 18, 1775; in Greene's Nathanael Greene (1867), vol. 1, p. 126.

[2] Washington's Writings (Ford), vol. 1, p. 81; vol. 3, p. 247.

The character and care of the private soldiers were subjects for debate in every town that labored diligently to keep its quota of men in the field. As the farmers sat about the fire in the stuffy town threshing the matter out, a weather-worn, weary volunteer home upon furlough often sat there too and heard what they thought of him. Sometimes he had an opportunity to know what the leaders thought. Elijah Fisher has described his interview with the committee of inquiry in Boston, whither he went to get satisfaction, having complained because they deducted from the amount still due him as wages on account of the depreciation in paper money, the bounty which he had received. The punctuation has been added, but the story is his:

"One of the Comita, start[ing] up, with his grate wigg, said the sholgers had been used very well; sometimes these things were not to be got, and then we could not have them as soon as we should wish. I was rong in acusing and talking as you [I?] do.

"Then spake up another, that set a little Distance and heard what was said (a black haired man), in my behalf, and said that the sholgers had been used very ill as this man said, and that

[42]

they are cheated out of a good eel that they ought to have. . . ." [1]

It was no light task to bring an army into the field and maintain it for years, combating successfully the local prejudices of northerner and southerner, the greed for bounties, the trials that follow a depreciating currency and an advance in the price of family necessities, the fear of militarism and the dislike of strict discipline in an age of democratic theories. That the army about Boston had the virtues that characterized many of the soldiers themselves no one will doubt. That it fell short in certain particulars may be surmised from the exclamation of a southern rifleman in the camp at Prospect Hill in September, 1775: " Such Sermons, such Negroes, such Colonels, such Boys, & such Great Great Grandfathers." [2]

[1] E. Fisher's Journal, p. 14.
[2] Letter of Jesse Lukens ; in Boston Public Library Historical Manuscripts, No. 1, p. 27.

II

Maintaining the Forces

WITH the opening of spring in the year 1776 (March 17th) the British evacuated Boston, and Washington was free to turn his attention to New York. The new field of action was far from the farms of many of the volunteers and they were anxious to be relieved from service; the people in the central colonies were by no means united in support of the patriot cause and army life among them was not found to be as pleasant as it had been in New England. The situation from a military point of view was more difficult than in Massachusetts, and Washington, learning his lessons as a commander in the school of experience, made life harder for the rank and file. Recruits were few, and there was need of some method to increase the army for the new enterprises.

Early in June Congress drew up a plan to enlist militia, 6,000 for the campaign in Canada, 13,800 for New York, and 10,000 for a flying camp in the middle colonies; but the bounty of

$10 which was offered had little effect upon men who could get a larger sum for shorter emergency service in the local organizations.[1]   Two other inducements were held out, a gift of land as suggested by Washington,[2] and a provision for soldiers who should be so injured that they could no longer serve in the army nor get their livelihood by their labor.[3]

A serious obstacle which confronted the eastern States at this time in their attempts to fill their quotas was an excessive rage for privateering which drew from New England alone some 10,000 hardy, brave men.   Clever advertisements in the newspapers[4] and alluring posters were handed about; these, with marvellous stories of spoils from the West Indies, repeated from mouth to mouth, fostered discontent in camp and checked enlistments at home.[5]   Vast numbers, said Mrs. Adams, were employed in privateering, and officers were not too particular in the methods used to get recruits away from the militia.[6]   Self-

[1] Journals of Congress, June 26, 1776.

[2] Washington's Writings (Ford), vol. 4, p. 380.

[3] Journals of Congress, August 26, 1776.

[4] Miss Caulkins's New London, p. 541.

[5] B. Rust to R. H. Lee; in American Archives V., vol. 3, col. 1513 ; also *ibid.*, vol. 2, col. 337.

[6] *Ibid.*, vol. 2, col. 599 ; col. 622.

interest, said John Paul Jones, and this only, influenced owners and sailors who preferred privateers to the navy service.[1] Looking at the matter in another way, privateers were a blessing; they offered protection to helpless seaport towns, and discouraged petty marauding expeditions of the British against fishing villages.   This work of the privateers freed the militia from service in the coastguard, and permitted a concentration of forces for larger undertakings.[2]

The prevalence of smallpox about Boston in the summer of 1776 added to the trials of Massachusetts recruiting officers, and made help from that section of the country less welcome to the army at New York;[3] but the need of reënforcements was so urgent that any risk seemed justifiable.   The effect of enlistments and drafts upon the population of a small town are described by Mrs. John Adams in September, 1776:

" Forty men," she writes, " are now drafted from this town.   More than one half, from sixteen to fifty, are now in the service. . . .   I hardly

---

[1] American Archives V., vol. 2, col. 1105.   See also Rhode Island Historical Society Collections, vol. 6, p. 207.

[2] James Lyon, in American Archives V., vol. 1, col. 1282.

[3] Serle to Lord Dartmouth, August 12th.   Stevens's Facsimiles, No. 2041.

GREAT
ENCOURAGEMENT
FOR
SEAMEN.

ALL GENTLEMEN SEAMEN and able-bodied LANDSMEN who have a Mind to distinguish themselves in the GLORIOUS CAUSE of their Country, and make their Fortunes, an Opportunity now offers on board the Ship RANGER, of twenty Guns, (for France) now laying in Portsmouth, in the State of New-Hampshire, commanded by JOHN PAUL JONES Esq; let them repair to the Ship's Rendezvous in Portsmouth, or at the Sign of Commodore Manley, in Salem, where they will be kindly entertained, and receive the greatest Encouragement.—The Ship Ranger, in the Opinion of every Person who has seen her is looked upon to be one of the best Cruisers in America.—She will be always able to Fight her Guns under a most excellent Cover; and no Vessel yet built was ever calculated for sailing faster, and making good Weather.

Any Gentlemen Volunteers who have a Mind to take an agreable Voyage in this pleasant Season of the Year, may, by entering on board the above Ship Ranger, meet with every Civility they can possibly expect, and for a further Encouragement depend on the first Opportunity being embraced to reward each one agreable to his Merit.

All reasonable Travelling Expences will be allowed, and the Advance-Money be paid on their Appearance on Board.

In CONGRESS, March 29, 1777.

RESOLVED,

THAT the Marine Committee be authorised to advance to every able Seaman, that enters into the Continental Service, any Sum not exceeding FORTY DOLLARS, and to every ordinary Seaman or Landsman, any Sum not exceeding TWENTY DOLLARS, to be deducted from their future Prize-Money.

By Order of CONGRESS,
JOHN HANCOCK, President.

DANVERS: Printed by E. Russell, at the House late the Bell-Tavern.

A very rare broadside inviting enlistment under Paul Jones, 1777.
(Original owned by the Essex Institute, Salem.)

think you can be sensible how much we are thinned in this Province. . . . If it is necessary to make any more drafts upon us, the women must reap the harvests. I am willing to do my part. I believe I could gather corn and husk it, but I should make a poor figure at digging potatoes."[1]

The absence of militiamen during harvest time was a serious loss to a town in the destruction of unharvested crops; the knowledge of this preyed upon the minds of the farmer-soldiers themselves and led to desertion.[2] " In some parishes," wrote Colonel Fitch, of Connecticut, "but one or two [men] are left; some have got ten or twelve loads of hay cut, and not a man left to take it up; some five or six, under the same circumstances; some have got a great quantity of grass to cut; some have not finished hoeing corn; some, if not all, have got all their ploughing to do, for sowing their winter grain; some have all their families sick, and not a person left to take care of them. . . . It is enough to make a man's heart ache to hear the complaints of some of them."[3]

---

[1] American Archives V., vol. 2, col. 599 (September 29th).
[2] *Ibid.*, vol. 1, col. 172.
[3] Jonathan Fitch to Governor Trumbull, August 13, 1776; in American Archives V., vol. 1, col. 938.

In the southern colonies the minds of the recruits from the frontier or "back country" were frequently harassed by rumors of Indian raids upon their homes. Officers at such times asked for furloughs or resigned, and privates deserted in their desperation.[1]

Under these circumstances the most pressing calls for more troops met with little response from the people. They felt that they had done enough, and the legislatures were either unwilling or unable to urge them to further sacrifice. If Congress itself was slow to see the need of a greater army, the disaster at Long Island in August produced an immediate change. Upon September 16th Congress voted that eighty-eight battalions be enlisted to serve during the war.[2] Each noncommissioned officer and private was promised a bounty of $20, and a hundred acres of land

[1] Salley's Orangeburg County, S. C., p. 439.

[2] The apportionment was :

New Hampshire..	3 battalions	Delaware	1 battalion
Massachusetts Bay.	15 "	Maryland	8 battalions
Rhode Island	2 "	Virginia	15 "
Connecticut	8 "	North Carolina.	9 "
New York	4 "	South Carolina.	6 "
New Jersey	4 "	Georgia	1 battalion
Pennsylvania.....	12 "		

Sixteen additional battalions were authorized later. (Heath's Memoirs, p. 116, and Journals of Congress, December 27th.)

In CONGRESS,

SEPTEMBER 16, 1776.

RESOLVED, That eighty-eight Battalions be enlisted as soon as possible, to serve during the present War, and that each State furnish their respective Quotas in the following Proportions, viz.

New-Hampshire	-	-	-	3	Battalions.
Massachusetts-Bay	-	-	-	15	Ditto.
Rhode-Island	-	-	-	2	Ditto.
Connecticut	-	-	-	8	Ditto.
New-York	-	-	-	4	Ditto.
New-Jersey	-	-	-	4	Ditto.
Pennsylvania	-	-	-	12	Ditto.
Delaware	-	-	-	1	Ditto.
Maryland	-	-	-	2	Ditto,
Virginia	-	-	-	15	Ditto.
North-Carolina	-	-	-	9	Ditto.
South-Carolina	-	-	-	6	Ditto.
Georgia	-	-	-	1	Ditto.

THAT Twenty Dollars be given as a Bounty to each non-commissioned Officer and private Soldier, who shall enlist to serve during the present War, unless sooner discharged by Congress.

THAT Congress make Provision for granting Lands in the following Proportions to the Officers and Soldiers who shall so engage in the Service, and continue therein to the Close of the War, or until discharged by Congress, and to the Representatives of such Officers and Soldiers as shall be slain by the Enemy; such Lands to be provided by the United States, and whatever Expence shall be necessary to procure such Land, the said Expence shall be paid and borne by the States in the same Proportion as the other Expences of the War, viz.

To a Colonel	-	-	500	Acres.
a Lieutenant-Colonel	-	-	450	Ditto.
a Major	-	-	400	Ditto.
a Captain	-	-	300	Ditto.
a Lieutenant	-	-	200	Ditto.
an Ensign	-	-	150	Ditto,

Each non-commissioned Officer and Soldier 100 Acres.

THAT the Appointment of all Officers and filling up Vacancies (except general Officers) be left to the Governments of the several States, and that every State provide Arms, Cloathing, and every Necessary for its Quota of Troops according to the foregoing Estimate; the Expence of the Cloathing to be deducted from the pay of the Soldiers as usual.

THAT all Officers be commissioned by Congress.

THAT it be recommended to the several States that they take the most speedy and effectual Measures for enlisting their several Quotas. That the Money to be given for Bounties be paid by the Paymaster in the Department where the Soldier shall enlist.

THAT each Soldier receive Pay and Subsistence from the Time of their Enlistment.

SEPTEMBER 18, 1776.

RESOLVED, That if Rations be received by the Officers or Privates in the Continental Army in Money, they be paid at the Rate of Eight Ninetieth Parts of a Dollar per Ration.

THAT the Bounty and Grants of Land, offered by Congress by a Resolution of the 16th Instant as an Encouragement to the Officers and Soldiers to engage to serve in the Army of the United States during the War, shall extend to all who are or shall be enlisted for that Term. The Bounty of Ten Dollars which any of the Soldiers have received from the Continent on Account of a former Enlistment, to be reckoned in part Payment of the Twenty Dollars offered by said Resolution.

THAT no Officer in the Continental Army is allowed to hold more than one Commission, or to receive Pay but in one Capacity.

SEPTEMBER 19, 1776.

THAT the Adjutants of Regiments in the Continental Army be allowed the Pay and Rations of Captains, and have the Rank of First Lieutenants.

IN order to prevent the Officers and Soldiers who shall be entitled to the Lands hereafter to be granted by the Resolution of Congress of the 16th, from disposing of the same during the War,

RESOLVED, That this Congress will not grant Lands to any Person or Persons claiming under the Assignment of an Officer or Soldier.

By Order of the CONGRESS,

JOHN HANCOCK, PRESIDENT.

Resolution of Congress to enlist 88 battalions.

were to be given to him, or to his representative if he was "slain by the enemy" before the close of the war. The expense necessary to procure the land was to be borne by the States in the same proportion as the other expenses of the war. The States were to provide arms, clothing, and every necessity, the cost of the clothing to be deducted from the pay of the men.[1] A little later, however, Congress voted a suit of clothes (or $20 if the soldier owned the clothes) to be given annually as a further inducement.[2] Washington in general orders November 10, 1776, announced that those who enlisted into the new army would have the usual pay and rations, but no boys or old men and no deserters would be received. At the same time the army regulations were repealed and a more rigorous code was put in force to bring the service to a higher standard of discipline.[3]

The plan to raise eighty-eight battalions, so simple on paper, developed endless complications. The States, as might be expected, found it diffi-

[1] Journals of Congress, September 16, 1776.

[2] *Ibid.*, October 8, 1776.

[3] American Archives V., vol. 2, col. 561. In November Gates's force numbered 11,526 men ; Lee had 10,768 men. (*Ibid.*, vol. 3, cols. 702, 710.) See also W. Eddis's Letters from America (1792), pp. 342, 343.

cult to fill their quotas, and they resorted to additional bounties; Connecticut and Massachusetts voted 20*s.* a month to privates above that allowed by Congress, and $33⅓ additional bounty; New Jersey offered $53⅓; Maryland objected to giving money in any case and wished to substitute land.[1] At a meeting of New England delegates to regulate prices the plea was made that Congress would not increase the pay of soldiers to meet high prices and a larger bounty was the last resort. Massachusetts then offered $86⅔, and New Hampshire did the same. In this confusion the bewildered recruits stood irresolute, hoping that bounties had but just begun their upward course. Meanwhile the eighty-eight battalions had to be filled by drafts of one man in four or five, excluding, however, those already in service, those in seaboard or frontier towns, school-masters, students, and a portion of those employed in powder-mills.[2] The men who

[1] Washington's Writings (Ford), vol. 5, pp. 18, 20, 213, *notes.*

[2] American Archives V., vol. 2, col. 763. Many who paid a fine rather than go when drafted received a receipt similar to the following : " Recd of Mr. Caleb Craft the Sum of Ten Pounds Lawfull Money in full for his fine he Refuseing to go a Solder when Draughted by the Town."—MS. in Brookline Public Library.

"abandoning his post" ordered to be cashiered.

The General approves each of the above sentences; orders the former to join their regiments; and the latter to depart the army immediately.

———

Head Quarters, White Plains, Nov. 9, 1776.

Parole —————— Countersign ——————

The General desires, that all Colonels and commanding Officers of regiments, will be particularly attentive, that no discharged men, or men whose times have or are about to expire, be suffered to carry off any Arms, Camp Kettles, Utensils, or any other kind of effect, which belong to the public; but that the whole be carefully delivered to the Quarter Master General, or his assistants; or to the Commissary of Stores, as the case may be, taking receipts therefor, in discharge of those they have signed for the delivery, in behalf of the Corps they respectively belong to.

———

Head Quarters, White Plains, Nov. 10, 1776.

Parole North Castle.   Countersign Bedford.

Such Officers as have been commissioned by the different States for the New Army, are immediately to set about enlisting from the troops of such State only, upon the following terms.

Twenty Dollars Bounty.
A Suit of Cloaths.
One hundred Acres of land.

The same pay and Rations, as are now given — The service to continue during

Orders relating to private soldiers.
Page from Washington's order book, Nov. 9, 1776.

served in the artillery—known as bombardiers and matrosses—held back so persistently that Washington was forced to offer an advance in pay of twenty-five per cent. to obtain the necessary numbers.[1]

The Continental army had its first time of serious privation in the winter that was just setting in; the soldiers in the northern camps especially deserve to share the fame that came to those who suffered and survived at Valley Forge a year later. A gentleman, writing from Ticonderoga December 4, 1776, concluded his letter with the words:

"For all this Army at this place, which did consist of twelve or thirteen thousand men, sick and well, no more than nine hundred pair of shoes have been sent. One third at least of the poor wretches is now barefoot, and in this condition obliged to do duty. This is shocking to humanity. It cannot be viewed in any milder light than black murder. The poor creatures is now (what's left alive) laying on the cold ground, in poor thin tents, and some none at all, and many down with the pleurisy. No barracks, no hospitals to go in. The barracks is at *Saratoga*. If you was here, your heart would melt. I paid a

[1] Washington's Writings (Ford), vol. 5, p. 113.

visit to the sick yesterday in a small house called a hospital. The first object presented [to] my eyes, one man laying dead at the door; the [n] inside two more laying dead, two living lying between them; the living with the dead had so laid for four-and-twenty hours. I went no further; this was too much to see and to much to feel, for a heart with the least tincture of humanity."[1]

To Ticonderoga the men had marched cheerfully, a great part of them barefooted and barelegged. In this condition they were forced to look forward to sentinel duty in the snow of a northern winter.[2] A British officer, in a letter dated at York Island, October 30, 1776, states that "the Rebel army are in so wretched a condition as to clothing and accoutrements, that I believe no nation ever saw such a set of tatterdemalions. There are few coats among them but what are out at elbows and in a whole regiment there is scarce a pair of breeches. Judge then how they must be pinched by a winter campaign."[3]

Such were the hardships endured by the army;

[1] Jos. Wood to Thomas Wharton, Jr.; in American Archives V., vol. 3, col. 1358.

[2] Richard Stockton, in *ibid.*, vol. 2, cols. 1274, 1275.

[3] American Archives V., vol. 2, col. 1293.

disease and cold thinned the ranks that had borne
the attack of British infantry. So great was the
demand for men that not a few deserted to reënlist,
and the temptation increased with the duration
of the war.[1] A punishment of a hundred lashes
had little effect, and in 1778 a man was shot who
had deserted and reënlisted for the bounties seven
times.[2] For him there was no semblance of excuse, but for some who went home without leave
a word in extenuation might be said. They received few of the blessings, usually, that the recruiting officer held before trusting eyes; they
lived for months without proper or even decent
food and clothing, fighting (in some cases) for a
country that had known them but a few years
and against friends and neighbors of their youth.[3]
If they had been drafted or had been induced to
sign enlistment papers when dazed by liquor,
their consciences did not hold them to service in
the army. Later on, an officer, after complaining
that the troops had been for two years without
clothes and pay, affirmed that there must have

[1] E. Wild's Diary ; in Massachusetts Historical Society Proceedings, October, 1890, p. 93.

[2] Orderly book of the Northern Army at Ticonderoga, p. 9.

[3] Colonel Richardson in September, 1775, spoke of the need
of arms to equip " the new Irish settlers " in South Carolina.—
Salley's Orangeburg County, S. C., p. 432.

been virtue in the army when under such circumstances there was any army left. A sentence in his diary which refers to a practice not uncommon in the early years of the war is good enough to bear repeating: "This day one of our soldiers which deserted some time ago deserted back again *with a new suit of cloaths*."[1]

Weak as the Continental army was in the autumn of 1776, it undertook two important duties; part of the forces held the Hudson above New York to check any advance of the British toward Canada or New England; another wing of the army kept to the banks of the Delaware to guard the highways to Pennsylvania and the south. On December 22d (just before the battle of Trenton was fought) the return of the army then encamped on the banks of the Delaware gives a total of 10,106 men; of these 3,357 were sick, absent on duty or on furlough, making thirty-three per cent. ineffective.[2] It was the current belief that affairs had come to a critical pass, requiring a successful battle to awaken enthusiasm and quicken

[1] W. McDowell's Journal; in Pennsylvania Archives, second series, vol. 15, p. 321. See also Army Correspondence of Colonel John Laurens, p. 139.

[2] American Archives V., vol. 3, col. 1401.

enlistments for the next campaign.[1] Washington's capture of nearly the whole British outpost at Trenton on Christmas night accomplished what was needed, but in order to follow up the success he was driven to a fresh bounty of $10 to keep the discontented men together for another month.

The year 1777, with its defeats at the Brandywine and at Germantown, brought little cheer to the main army until the news of Burgoyne's surrender came in October. Throughout the summer Washington never had above 11,000 Continentals and 2,000 militia in the field at one time. At the close of July Congress abandoned the expensive and unsatisfactory system of appointing army officers as recruiting agents; the States were to be divided into districts, with a local officer in each district, who was to receive $8 for every man enlisted and $5 for each deserter secured.[2] Washington expressed approval of an annual draft of men to fill the regiments that became reduced by death, disease, or the withdrawal of those who could not be induced by a bounty of $25 to remain in the service beyond the term of enlistment.[3]

[1] American Archives, V., vol. 3, col. 1514.
[2] Washington's Writings (Ford), vol. 6, p. 7.
[3] *Ibid.*, vol. 6, p. 305.

At the beginning of autumn the army, numbering some ten or eleven thousand men, marched through Front Street, Philadelphia, on the way to check the advance of General Howe. Alexander Graydon stood at the coffee-house corner and watched them pass, the Commander-in-chief and his men. They were, he says, indifferently dressed, but carried their well-burnished arms like good soldiers who might reasonably expect success in a contest with equal numbers. They were obliged to fall back a few days later before Knyphausen's advance over Brandywine Creek at Chadd's Ford and Cornwallis's flank attack by way of Birmingham church, greatly outnumbered but not put to rout.[1] General Howe occupied Philadelphia and thus achieved one object in the British plan of campaign. While the moral effect of this move was considerable at the time, Philadelphia being the great port of trade of the middle colonies, and a centre for army supplies of all kinds, he had, however, done little harm to Washington, and he now found that he must divide his army in order to protect both Philadelphia and New York. To put down the rebellion of an agricultural people, scattered over a wide territory, by a garrison in each town would have required more soldiers than

[1] Graydon's Memoirs, p. 291.

[56]

England possessed. The other movement of the year, Burgoyne's attempt to isolate New England by seizing Lake Champlain and the Hudson, which taken together formed a natural western barrier, ended in his capitulation.

Washington looked forward to winter quarters where the men could be near enough to the scene of action to furnish comfort to supporters of the patriot cause, where they could be drilled by Baron Steuben, and could be so fed and protected from the weather that sickness and desertion would not destroy the army. It seemed necessary to be at least a day's march from the enemy to afford time for defensive measures or for retreat in case the British made a hostile move. He therefore withdrew up the eastern bank of the Schuylkill some miles to the northwest of Philadelphia, crossed the river on December 13th by two bridges, one old and insecure and another improvised from boats and fence-rails, and on the 19th went into camp at Valley Forge. By January 1st most of the troops were settled in huts, and they soon began to improve in discipline under the instruction of Baron Steuben, who toiled with the zeal of "a lieutenant anxious for promotion."[1]

[1] Army Correspondence of Colonel John Laurens (1867), pp. 90–97, 100, 152, 160, 169.

The sufferings of the Continentals at Valley Forge during the winter of 1777–78, without sufficient clothing, blankets, or shoes, and much of the time destitute of proper food, are described in a succeeding chapter.

An army of about 17,000 men had melted away, until now, in 1778, 5,000 ragged soldiers remained. A Tory writer reported in March that 1,134 deserters had come into Philadelphia and taken the oath of allegiance. It is worthy of notice, in support of Washington's frequent request for recruits of American birth, that just three-fourths of these deserters were foreign born.[1] The effective force was further decreased by the pernicious habit of employing privates as officers' servants. Steuben has mentioned as an illustration of the system a certain company which had "twelve men present; absent, one man as valet to the commissary, two hundred miles distant from the army, for eighteen months; one man valet to a quartermaster attached to the army of the north, for twelve months; four in the different hospitals for so many months; two as drivers of carriages; and so many more as bakers, blacksmiths, carpenters, even as coal-porters, for years together." These men, once on the rolls,

[1] Joseph Galloway. Stevens's Facsimiles, No. 2094.

were reported regularly as part of the effective
force.[1]

With the opening of the spring campaign Congress called upon the States to maintain their
quotas,[2] and in May resolved to grant $80 at the
end of the war to every non-commissioned officer
and private who had enlisted or would enlist for
or during the contest.[3] In August it was reported
that "a great spirit of inlisting" had taken place
among the militia drafts.[4] A proposition to pay
part of the usual bounty of $20 in specie instead
of bills would have helped the movement along,
but on a vote it was lost, and an appropriation of
$120,000 in Continental money was made.[5] The

[1] Kapp's Steuben, p. 116. Also Baron de Kalb's views;
Stevens's Facsimiles, No. 761.

[2] See table, p. 48, *note*. Rhode Island was to furnish 1 battalion, New York 5, and Pennsylvania 10 ; South Carolina and
Georgia were omitted.—Journals of Congress, February 26,
1778.

[3] *Ibid.*, May 15, 1778.

[4] No soldier in the infantry battalions could—by a resolve of
August 31, 1778—enlist outside the battalions credited to the
State for which he had enlisted as a militiaman.

[5] The establishment of 1778 allowed to each battalion of infantry 477 privates with pay at $62⅔ per month ; artillery,
336 matrosses at $8⅓ per month ; cavalry, 324 dragoons,
$8⅓ per month ; provost, 43 provosts or privates, $8⅓ per
month ; three companies in the engineering department, each to
have sixty privates at $8⅓ per month (Journals of Congress

much - desired consummation of treaties with France was hailed with celebrations in the army, and the virtual victory at Monmouth following Clinton's evacuation of Philadelphia served in a sense to offset the loss of Savannah, which was not known in camp until the new year came in.

The opening weeks of 1779 disclosed conditions that might well have discouraged Washington himself. Congress authorized him to offer a bounty not to exceed $200 (in addition to the usual bounties of clothing, and, at the expiration of the war, of land and money) to be given to each man engaged for the war.[1] Later, where the bounty offered by a State exceeded $200, this sum was ordered to be put to the State's credit for each recruit furnished, to prevent the jealousies that might otherwise arise from too great inequality in the amount of

May 27, 1778). A regiment of infantry had 1 colonel (who was also a captain), 1 lieutenant-colonel (also captain), 1 major (also captain), 6 captains, paymaster, adjutant, quartermaster, 1 surgeon, 1 surgeon's mate, 8 lieutenants, 9 ensigns, 1 sergeant-major, 1 quartermaster-sergeant, 27 sergeants, 1 captain-lieutenant (over the colonel's company), 1 drum-major, 1 fife-major, 18 drums and fifes, 27 corporals, 477 privates : in all 585.

[1] Journals of Congress, January 23, 1779.

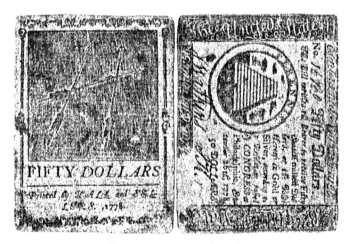

Paper currency, 1776, 1778.

bounty to be had when the national and local bounties were combined.[1] Washington already began to fear that the enlistments would prove a failure unless the State rivalry in offering large bounties was brought to an end. New Jersey offered $250 over and above the bounty voted by Congress; Georgia offered $300, and Virginia promised clothes, land, and $750 to recruits.[2] Naturally these sums, in spite of the depreciation in paper bills, made the soldiers who had enlisted earlier to serve for the whole war uneasy and vexed that they had accepted a paltry $20. Congress perceived this and allowed $100 to each man who had enlisted for the war previous to January 23, 1779.[3]

"You may," wrote the Commander-in-chief in July, "form a pretty good judgment of my prospect of a brilliant campaign, and of the figure I shall cut in it, when I inform you, that, excepting about 400 recruits from the State of Massachusetts (a portion of which I am told are children, hired at about 1500 dollars each for 9 months' service), I have had no reënforcements to this army since last

[1] Journals of Congress, March 9, 1779. There were to be eighty battalions of infantry.

[2] Washington's Writings (Ford), vol. 7, pp. 364–366.

[3] Journals of Congress, June 22, 1779.

campaign."[1] Some months earlier the Baron de
Kalb had said that so long as the substitutes hired
by rich citizens for the militia could get enormous
bounties for a "two months' walk"—as the short
enlistment was called—there was no hope for the
regular regiments.[2]

In October Washington's force engaged for the
war amounted to 14,998 men; to these must be
added 12,101 men engaged for short periods,
making in all 27,099, of whom 410 were invalids.[3] In the meantime the towns throughout
the country were approaching the end of their resources in their ability to furnish recruits.   Town
meeting followed town meeting to fill quotas of
men and provide beef, clothing, and fire-arms.
Training-bands and alarm-lists were scrutinized
for recruits, and at meetings attendance was secured by a threat to draft first from those who remained away from these deliberations.[4] In Massachusetts, which still furnished nearly a fifth of
the infantry battalions, the towns finally were
divided into as many classes as there were men to

[1] Washington's Writings (Ford), vol. 7, p. 505.
[2] De Kalb to De Broglie, December, 1777 ; Stevens's Facsimiles, No. 761.
[3] Washington's Writings (Ford), vol. 8, p. 111.
[4] Parmenter's Pelham, pp. 142–148.

be raised, each class to furnish and pay for a man, or pay the average price paid for Continental soldiers, with twenty-five per cent. added.[1] Somewhat earlier, in Connecticut, any two men were exempted from draft so long as they could keep a recruit in the field—a practice that led to the employment of negroes and lowered the grade of recruits.[2]

The success of the recruiting service varied according to local conditions, and particularly where the people were influenced by frequent reports from the army. *Rivington's Gazette*, April 17, 1779, stated that the rebels, who were fed with putrid salt beef and wretched whiskey, were ready to desert from a service which they despised and detested; while the *New Hampshire Gazette* ten days later reported that there was a great eagerness to enlist, that nine-tenths of the southern forces, being pleased with their food and their superior clothing, had reënlisted. Nearly all newspaper statements of the time were more or less inaccurate and intemperate; and the information made public by British and American editors, and par-

[1] Resolves General Court of Massachusetts, February 26, 1781 ; Town Records Pelham, Brookline, etc.

[2] Massachusetts Historical Society Proceedings, August, 1862, p. 198.

ticularly the loyalist editors, was colored beyond recognition.

For several years Indians and Tories from the lake region in central New York had harried the frontier settlements in Washington's rear. The Indians kept under cultivation some 20,000 acres of corn and thousands of fruit-trees, inhabiting the rich lands from Lake Ontario at the north to Tioga Point, the meeting-place of the Chemung River with the Susquehanna, just within the bounds of Pennsylvania, on the south. In the summer of 1779 General James Clinton started from Schenectady by way of Otsego Lake and its outlet the upper Susquehanna to meet General John Sullivan, who marched northward from Easton along the Lehigh River and the lower Susquehanna. They joined forces at Tioga Point, and late in August drove the British and their savage allies from their stronghold on the Chemung, near the present city of Elmira. The devastation which followed put an end to the great Indian highway between Canada and the Chesapeake, dispersed the enemy that menaced Washington in the rear, and left him free to face Sir Henry Clinton's army.[1]

[1] See Chapter IX. ; also W. E. Griffis in New England Magazine, December, 1900.

A careful French *résumé* of the situation concludes with the opinion that affairs were alarming but not desperate in the autumn of 1779: that the country, like a convalescent, needed nourishment rather than medicine, and a careful nurse rather than a physician.[1]

The year 1780, with the loss of Charleston, the defeat at Camden, and the treason of Arnold, seemed to portend surrender at last. But forces were at work that were to outweigh them all in the fortunes of war; in France the colonies grew in favor, and the French fleet appeared upon the American coast; in England, now at war with France and Spain, the King's policy was about to add Holland to the circle of her enemies; while in the colonies the Continentals, under the eye of that indefatigable disciplinarian, the Baron Steuben, grew into an army of hardy, patient, and obedient soldiers.[2] There were 10,400 rank and file that spring on the North River to oppose a British force of 11,000. Washington asked for fifty regiments or 35,850 men.[3] Congress had

[1] Stevens's Facsimiles, No. 1616.

[2] *Ibid.*, Nos. 1627, 1632.

[3] Washington's Writings (Ford), vol. 8, p. 235; *ibid.*, vol. 8, p. 487; Journals of Congress, October 3, 21, 1780 (change in regiments).

already lost much of the prestige which made its wish effective in 1775, and as it had ceased to exercise the right to issue paper money, it could " neither enlist, pay, nor feed a single soldier; " the Commander was obliged to rely largely upon his own efforts to rouse the country.[1] Had Congress supported with courage despotic laws similar to those enacted eighty-four years later by the Confederate Congress it is possible that the people would have held that the occasion justified the action.   To enlarge its force in the field the Confederacy employed free negroes and slaves in every position at home and in camp where a white man could thereby be released for army duty. By an act of February 17, 1864, every white resident between the ages of seventeen and fifty became at its passage a part of the military service of the Confederate States until the end of the war.

The condition of Washington's army in the autumn of 1780 was so disheartening that a hostile observer could hardly over-color the picture of ragged, half-fed battalions, thinned by desertion, disease, and expirations of terms of service. Benedict Arnold, the traitor of less than two

[1] Madison to Jefferson, May 6, 1780 ; in his Writings (Hunt), vol. 1, p. 63.

FOR the Encouragement of thofe that fhall I[nlift]
in the Continental Army—The CONGRESS in
their Refolves of *September* 16th, 18th, 19th, *October*
8th, and *November* 12th, 1776, Engage,

THAT *Twenty Dollars* be given as a Bounty to each Non-Commiffioned Offic[er] and Private Soldier who fhall Inlift to ferve for the Term
of Three Years.

That each Non-Commiffioned Officer and private Soldier fhall annually
receive a Suit of Cloaths, to confift for the prefent Year, of Two Linnen
Hunting Shirts, Two Pair of Overalls, a Leathern or Woolen Waiftcoat with
Sleeves, One Pair of Breeches, a Hat or Leather Cap, Two Shirts, Two Pair
of Hofe, and Two Pair of Shoes, amounting in the whole to the Value of
Twenty Dollars, or that Sum to be paid to each Soldier who fhall procure
thofe Articles for himfelf, and produces a Certificate thereof from the Captain
of the Company to which he belongs, to the Pay Mafter of the Regiment.

That each Non-Commiffioned Officer and private Soldier who fhall Inlift
and engage to continue in the Service to the Clofe of the War, or until dif-
charged by CONGRESS, fhall receive in Addition to the above Encouragement, ONE HUNDRED ACRES OF LAND, and if any are Slain by the Enemy, the Reprefentatives of fuch Soldiers fhall be intitled to the aforefaid Hundred Acres of Land.

And for their further Encouragement, the State of *Maffachufetts-Bay*, has,
by a Refolve of *November* 2[?], engaged;

That each Non Commiffioned Officer, and private Soldier who fhall Inlift
into the Continental Army, either during the War, or for the Term of Three
Years, a Part of the Quota of Men affigned this State, the Sum of *Twenty
Pounds* on his paffing Mufter, the faid *Twenty Pounds* to be paid in Treafur-
er's Notes of *Ten Pounds* each, payable to the Poffeffor in Four Years, with
Intereft to be paid annually, at the Rate of *Six per Cent.*

In the Houfe of REPRESENTATIVES, Dec. 4, 1776.

THE foregoing Extracts were Read and Ordered to be Printed.

JAMES WARREN, Speaker.

Enlistment broadside.

weeks' standing under His Majesty's protection,
has described the army of 11,400 men, half of
whom, the militia, would return to their homes
on January 1st. These men, " illy clad, badly
fed, and worse paid, having in general two or
three years' pay due to them," were the result
of an appeal for 35,000 soldiers who were to
drive Sir Henry Clinton out of New York and
end the war. The public debt, he added, amounted to 400,000,000 paper dollars; and Congress,
jealous of the army and powerless over the States,
could do little. Provisions were of necessity
taken from the people and this swelled the tide
of discontent. Arnold's picture of the army was
drawn from a knowledge of the facts scarcely
inferior to Washington's own.[1] The mutiny of
the Pennsylvania line at the beginning of the
new year resulted naturally from these conditions.

A plan for the reduction of the regular army
after January 1, 1781, to four regiments of dragoons or cavalry, four of artillery, forty-nine of
infantry (with 612 men in each), exclusive of
Colonel Hazen's regiment, Colonel Armand's
partisan corps, Major Lee's corps, and one regi-

[1] Benedict Arnold's Present State of the American Rebel
Army (Winnowings in American History; Revolutionary nar-
ratives, No. 5).

ment of artificers,[1] was approved by Congress in October, 1780; little was accomplished in this direction until near the end of the war.

Morgan's victory over Tarleton at the Cowpens in January, 1781, was followed by the defeat of Greene at Guilford, Hobkirk's Hill, and Eutaw Springs. But these seemingly unfortunate incidents in Greene's masterly Southern Campaign were soon to be overshadowed by the siege of Lord Cornwallis's army at Yorktown,

---

[1] Journals of Congress, October 3, 21, 1780. The quotas were : New Hampshire : two regiments of infantry. Massachusetts : ten of infantry, one of artillery. Rhode Island : one of infantry. Connecticut : five of infantry, one of cavalry. New York : two of infantry, one of artillery. New Jersey : two of infantry. Pennsylvania : six of infantry, one of artillery, one of cavalry, one of artificers. Delaware : one of infantry. Maryland : five of infantry. Virginia : eight of infantry, one of artillery, two of cavalry. North Carolina : four of infantry. South Carolina : two of infantry. Georgia : one of infantry. Every recruit enlisted for the war was to receive a sum not exceeding $50. All the foreigners in the service of the United States were brought together in Colonel Hazen's regiment. August 7, 1782, the Secretary of War was instructed by Congress to see that each regiment was completed to not less than 500 rank and file, and that the reduction in the number of regiments ordered in 1780 was carried out. Such of the sixteen additional regiments as were not annexed to the line of their particular states and all separate light corps and the German battalion were to be struck from the establishment.

and the surrender which came in October. The cessation of active hostilities was very welcome to America, although defensive measures were by no means exhausted. Washington and Greene had come to know the strategic possibilities of the country which lies between the mountains and the Atlantic coast. The broad rivers that everywhere flow southerly and easterly to the sea formed barriers, and the long stretches of sparsely inhabited country seriously hindered the operations of an invading commander who struck inland for any distance from his ships. While the struggle was waged now in the eastern, now in the central, now in the southern colonies, great tracts of land could be cultivated in comparative peace, regardless of a depreciating currency, an anxious Congress, or a ragged army. The recruiting officer was the only reminder of strife that came into many a quiet cabin in the forest clearing.[1] With the seed planted or the grain gathered men were ready to shoulder their muskets for a short campaign, just as the Scotch Highlanders waited for the autumn harvests before raiding the lowlands.

In the spring of 1782 the British House of Commons declared that all who should advise

[1] Channing's United States (New York, 1896), pp. 77-79.

the further prosecution of offensive war in America would be considered as enemies to his Majesty and the country. The Continental military establishment at this time was in the neighborhood of 35,000 men, with an effective French force of 4,000 troops. The British establishment, including detachments at Charleston, Savannah, Halifax, on the Penobscot and in Canada, with the militia at New York, was supposed to be about 26,000 men.[1] The resignation of Lord North in March and the signing of preliminary articles between Great Britain and the United States in November prepared the way for a cessation of hostilities early in 1783. On April 19th peace was announced to the soldiers by Washington.

The days of trial were over for the army which, in the Commander's words, was of nearly eight years' standing. Six years they had spent in the field without any other shelter from the inclemency of the seasons than tents, or such houses as they could build for themselves without expense to the public. They had encountered hunger, cold, and nakedness. They had fought many battles and bled freely. They had lived without pay, and in consequence of it, officers as well as

[1] Washington's Writings (Ford), vol. 9, p. 468.

[70]

men had subsisted upon their rations. They had often, very often, been reduced to the necessity of eating salt pork, or beef, not for a day or a week only, but for months together, without vegetables or money to buy them.[1]

During these eight dark years the officers and men who served under Washington grew more and more to know that a great man led them. In correspondence, in journals, and in the conversation of visitors who had come from Europe, the Commander of the Continental Army was mentioned with a regard rarely if ever before bestowed during life upon the central figure of a bitter war for independence. His letters were preserved by the families of British officers;[2] and the British historian, John Richard Green, with rare comprehension of his character, has said of him: "No nobler figure ever stood in the forefront of a nation's life. Washington was grave and courteous in address; his manners were simple and unpretending; his silence and the serene calmness of his temper spoke of a perfect self-mastery. . . . It was only as the weary fight went on that the colonists discovered, however slowly and im-

[1] From Washington's words, in his Writings (Ford), vol. 10, p. 204.
[2] De Fonblanque's Burgoyne (1876), p. 329, note.

[71]

perfectly, the greatness of their leader, his clear judgment, his heroic endurance, his silence under difficulties, his calmness in the hour of danger or defeat, the patience with which he waited, the quickness and hardness with which he struck, the lofty and serene sense of duty that never swerved from its task through resentment or jealousy, that never through war or peace felt the touch of a meaner ambition, that knew no aim save that of guarding the freedom of his fellow-countrymen, and no personal longing save that of returning to his own fireside when their freedom was secured. It was almost unconsciously that men learned to cling to Washington with a trust and faith such as few other men have won, and to regard him with a reverence which still hushes us in presence of his memory." [1]

[1] Green's History of the English People (New York, 1880), vol. 4, pp. 254, 255 (Book IX., chapter ii.).

III
Material Needs

A COLUMN of infantry in a country highway, giving a touch of color and life to
the landscape, might well fire the pulse
of any lad; and at the opening of the Revolution
the glamour of military service, supplementing
as it did the patriotic spirit, caused the volunteer
army about Boston to increase in numbers from
day to day, coming from the hills and plains, until
the British looked out upon a besieging camp.
But experience, as it ever does, cooled the pulse
and cleared the brain; then the country boy
began to examine the soldier's knapsack and
the size of his blanket.[1] Washington shows in
his Revolutionary correspondence that he knew
these simple things, and when mutiny and desertion alarmed the colonies he sought the only
permanent remedy—a greater degree of comfort
for his men.

[1] Dr. A. Waldo's Diary; in Historical Magazine, May,
1861, p. 130.

The soldier's bed was often under the stars of heaven or the clouds of a threatening storm. If he was fortunate enough to possess a tent he fared better, but did not always escape the rain. The conversation recorded by a Connecticut surgeon expresses a condition which was far too frequent.

"Good - morning, brother soldier, how are you?"

"All wet, I thank 'e," says the other; "hope you are so."[1]

When the sun reappeared after a storm, tents were struck for a few hours to let the ground dry, and were pitched again at nightfall.[2]   Few troops had suitable covering at the camp in Cambridge in 1775, except the troops from Rhode Island; their tents were, according to Rev. Mr. Emerson, "in the most exact English style."[3]   For the most part the shelters were as dissimilar in form as the men were in dress, and each one was somewhat of an index to the character of its owner; some were of boards, and others of sail-cloth, some a combi-

[1] Dr. A. Waldo's Diary; in Historical Magazine, May, 1861, p. 132.

[2] Orderly book, Pennsylvania State Regiment, Pennsylvania Magazine, January, 1899, p. 477.

[3] Washington's Writings (Sparks), vol. 3, p. 491.   MS. letter quoted.

nation of both, while stones, brush, and turf were forced into service.[1]

Huts built of fence-rails, sod, and straw could not be moved to dry or clear the ground, but they were in winter warmer than tents.[2] Boards were used for floors when they were to be had, and also for the construction of the huts if there was a saw-mill near the camp; otherwise logs did duty, as in pioneer days, with the interstices filled with clay, moss, or straw.[3] Each hut was supposed to have two windows; it could be built in about two weeks, and the company officers not infrequently lent a hand.[4] In rude cabins like these, arranged in lines which extended back from the Schuylkill about one and a half miles,[5] the greater part of Washington's army passed the winter months at Valley Forge, beset from

[1] Washington's Writings (Sparks), vol. 3, p. 492. In October, 1776, "country linen fit for tents," a yard wide, sold for three shillings and sixpence a yard. Twenty-one and a half yards were required to make a tent for six men.— American Archives V., vol. 2, col. 988.

[2] *Ibid.*, vol. 2, col. 610.

[3] T. Anburey's Travels, vol. 2, p. 294.

[4] Washington's Revolutionary Orders (Whiting), p. 86, May 14, 1778. Dr. Waldo's Diary, Historical Magazine, May, 1861, p. 133.

[5] T. Blake's Journal, in Kidder's First New Hampshire Regiment, p. 40.

without by sleet and wind, from within by heat and smoke, until the eyes of the men smarted almost beyond endurance.[1]

The situation of the camp had much to do with the health and comfort of the men. Five sarcastic reasons for the selection of Valley Forge as a place in which to pass the winter of 1777-78 are worthy of record:

    1st. There is plenty of wood & water.
    2dly. There are but few families for the soldiery to steal from—tho' far be it from a soldier to steal—

[1] The following lines, written by Dr. Waldo at Valley Forge, April 26, 1778, describe a rather better hut than those used by the privates:

<blockquote>
Of pondrous logs
Whose bulk disdains the winds or fogs
The sides and ends are fitly raised
And by dove-tail each corner's brac'd:
Athwart the roof, young saplings lie
Which fire and smoke has now made dry—
Next, straw wraps o'er the tender pole,
Next earth, then splints o'erlay the whole;
Although it leaks when show'rs are o'er,
It did not leak two hours before.
Two chimneys plac'd at op'site angles
Keep smoke from causing oaths and wrangles.
  .   .   .   .   .

Three windows, placed all in sight,
Through oiled paper give us light;
One door, on wooden hinges hung,
Lets in the friend, or sickly throng.
</blockquote>

—Historical Magazine, September, 1863, p. 270.

[76]

[3dly not given.]

4ly. There are warm sides of hills to erect huts on.

5ly. They will be heavenly minded like Jonah when in the belly of a great Fish.

6ly. They will not become home sick as is sometimes the case when men live in the open world —since the reflections which must naturally arise from their present habitation, will lead them to the more noble thoughts of employing their leisure hours in filling their knapsacks with such materials as may be necessary on the Jorney to another Home.[1]

Dressing and the morning meal were events which varied in importance, for at times there was little to wear and less to eat. In the campaign about Whitemarsh, in December, 1777, a soldier remarked: "We had no tents, nor anithing to Cook our Provisions in, and that was Prity Poor, for beef was very leen and no salt, nor any way to Cook it but to throw it on the Coles and brile it; and the warter we had to Drink and to mix our flower with was out of a brook that run along by the Camps, and so many a dippin and washin [in] it which maid it very Dirty and muddy."[2]

[1] Dr. Waldo's Diary, Historical Magazine, May, 1861, p. 131.

[2] Elijah Fisher's Journal, p. 7.

The cooking was often done by soldiers from each company, for men who had skill in any direction were soon called upon to perform special service. "Nothing remarkable this day," a private relates, "onely I was chose cook for our room consisting of 12 men, and a hard game too."[1] Sometimes there were no more than two kettles in which to prepare the meals for a company; the meat was broiled over the fire, spitted on a bayonet, and the bread was baked in the hot ashes.[2] The men counted themselves fortunate if they could dine in peace; at the siege of Boston a man was quietly eating his bread and milk when a cannon-ball struck near by and so covered the bowl with flying dirt that he could eat no more.[3]

The following daily allowance or ration was authorized by the third Provincial Congress, June 10, 1775:

1. One pound of bread.
2. Half a pound of beef and half a pound of pork; and if pork cannot be had, one pound and a

[1] Military Journals of Two Private Soldiers, p. 79 (references are to that by S. Haws).

[2] E. Wild's Journal, p. 29; same in Massachusetts Historical Society Proceedings, October, 1890, p. 104.

[3] Rev. B. Boardman's Diary, Massachusetts Historical Society Proceedings, May, 1892, p. 406.

quarter of beef; and one day in seven they shall have one pound and one quarter of salt fish, instead of one day's allowance of meat.

3. One pint of milk, or, if milk cannot be had, one gill of rice.

4. One quart of good spruce or malt beer.

5. One gill of peas or beans, or other sauce equivalent.

6. Six ounces of good butter per week.

7. One pound of good common soap for six men per week.

8. Half a pint of vinegar per week per man, if it can be had.[1]

During the siege of Boston all allowances for the week were delivered on Wednesday unless

[1] Journals of Each Provincial Congress (Lincoln), pp. 317, 318. In August, 1775, each soldier was granted 1 pound of fresh beef or ¾ pound of pork, or 1 pound of salt fish per diem; 1 pound of bread or flour per diem; 3 pints of peas or beans per week, or vegetables equivalent at 5 shillings sterling per bushel for peas or beans; 1 pint of milk per diem per man, when to be had; ½ pint of rice, or 1 pint of Indian meal, per man per week; 1 quart of spruce beer per man per diem, or 9 gallons of molasses per company of 100 men; 3 pounds of candles to 100 men per week, for guards, etc.; 24 pounds of soft or 8 pounds of hard soap for 100 men per week; 1 ration of salt, 1 ration of fresh meat, and 2 rations of bread, to be delivered Monday morning; Wednesday morning the same; Friday morning the same, and 1 ration of salt fish. Substantially the same ration was approved by Congress November 4, 1775, but with "or cider" after the word "beer."

the number of regiments made it necessary to serve a part of the army on other days.[1] In the winter months corned beef and pork were given out four days a week, a pound and a half of the former and eighteen ounces of the latter per diem. Onions at two and eightpence a bushel and potatoes or turnips at one and fourpence a bushel might be substituted for peas or beans.[2]

The ration authorized by Washington at Valley Forge in the spring of 1778 called for 1 1/2 pounds of flour or bread, 1 pound of beef or fish, or 3/4 pound of pork, and 1 gill of whiskey or spirits; or 1 1/2 pounds of flour, 1/2 pound of pork or bacon, 1/2 pint of peas or beans, and 1 gill of

[1] Colonel William Henshaw's Orderly Book, August 8, 1775, p. 66. The ration in force at the outbreak of the Spanish-American war of 1898 was: 1 1/4 pounds of beef or 3/4 pound of pork, 18 ounces of bread or flour, $\frac{1}{16}$ pound of coffee, $\frac{1.6}{100}$ pound of sugar, 1 pound of vegetables; 2 quarts of salt, 4 quarts of vinegar, 4 ounces of pepper, 4 pounds of soap, 1 1/2 pounds of candles, to 100 rations. An allowance at the rate of 60 cents per day per man was made for special food for the sick. In Cuba, however, the sick were fortunate if they received the army ration, when their comrades lived on hard bread, poor beef, coffee, sugar, and an occasional tomato.—Commissary-General of Subsistence, Report for year ending June 30, 1898, pp. 7, 25–32.

[2] Washington's Orders, December 24, 1775 ; also Barriger's Legislative History of Subsistence Department, second edition, p. 8.

whiskey or spirits. These amounts were varied according to the state of the stores in camp.[1]

Washington, writing to the president of Congress, June 28, 1776, estimated the cost of a ration at eightpence York currency, or a trifle more.[2] In the report of the committee on the commissary department, agreed to by Congress June 10, 1777, a ration was to be considered as worth ten ninetieths of a dollar, or a little over eleven cents.[3] When the army was in camp a market was established, where farmers were allowed to offer their produce for sale; and one suttling booth was permitted within each brigade's limits where liquor might be sold at fixed prices.[4] Milk was brought in from the country for the sick whenever it could be had, but the exorbitant sums asked by farmers were a frequent source of vexation and privation. At Peekskill General Putnam in 1777 fixed the prices of provisions, and made the penalty for buying articles at prices above those

[1] Washington's Revolutionary Orders (Whiting, 1844), p. 63.

[2] Washington's Writings (Ford), vol. 4, p. 185. The Virginia Committee of Safety in 1776 considered their ration of bacon, pork or beef, with flour or meal, and salt, worth 7½d. —Virginia Calendar of State Papers, vol. 8, p. 84.

[3] Barriger's Legislative History, second edition, p. 17.

[4] Washington's Revolutionary Orders (Whiting), p. 62.

authorized, the forfeiture of the produce or the value in money. Later, when milk could not be obtained at sixpence a quart, an officer and thirty men were detailed from each regiment to collect cows sufficient in number to supply the needs of the army, and to care for them until the owners would agree to the terms fixed by the general.[1]

The army often suffered from the scarcity of vegetables because perishable food could not be carried as readily as beef. In Sullivan's campaign against the Six Nations of Indians the men fared well; nuts and melons are mentioned in many diaries, and also corn or maize, which was ripe when the invading columns reached the first Indian villages. After corn became too old to boil or roast it was converted into meal; tin kettles, found in the red men's huts, were perforated and used to grate the kernels, and every fourth man not on guard, it is said, sat up at night to play the part of miller. This meal was mixed with hot pumpkin or boiled squash, and kneaded

[1] Putnam's Orders, August 8, 13, 1777. The prices were: Butter 2s. per pound; mutton and lamb, 8d.; veal 6d.; milk, 6d. per quart; potatoes 6s. per bushel; squashes, 1s. per peck; beans or peas in pod, 1s. 6d. per peck; cucumbers, 1s. per dozen; pig for roasting, 1s. per pound; turnips, carrots, and beets, 6s. per bushel, New York money. September 3; cider, 6d. York or 4d. lawful money per quart.

into cakes which were baked in the coals.[1] Food of this kind was of great importance in preventing the diseases which arise from a steady diet of meat. So great occasionally was the need of vegetables that a commander felt justified in ordering each regiment to prepare ground and plant seed, on the chance that head-quarters would not be moved before the time of harvest.[2] Congress, meanwhile, urged the colonies to encourage agricultural societies.[3]

When provisions were scarce the allowance per man was reduced sometimes to ½ pound of flour a day, ½ pound of beef, with 5 gills of salt to 100 pounds of beef.[4] At times the soldiers had no vinegar, at other times no vegetables or bread. In the midst of distracting quarrels among jealous officers, Washington sent out appeals for aid, writing: "Our soldiers the greatest part of last campaign, and the whole of this, have scarcely tasted any kind of vegetables; had but little salt

[1] Nathan Davis's History, Historical Magazine, April, 1868, p. 203.

[2] Putnam's General Orders, August 25, 1777, p. 62; also American Archives V., vol. 3, col. 1584.

[3] Journals of Congress, March 21, 1776.

[4] Dr. Jabez Campfield's Diary, p. 133; also Orderly Book of the Northern Army at Ticonderoga and Mt. Independence (Albany, 1859), p. 132.

and vinegar, which would have been a tolerable substitute for vegetables; have been in a great measure strangers to, neither have they been provided with, proper drink. Beer or cyder seldom comes within the verge of the camp, and rum in much too small quantities. Thus, to devouring large quantities of animal food, untemper'd by vegetables or vinegar, or by any kind of drink but water, and eating indifferent bread . . . are to be ascribed the many putrid diseases incident to the army."[1] In the winter of 1779 and 1780 the army was sometimes for five or six days without bread, often as long without meat, and once or twice two or three days without either.[2]

Men in the Arnold expedition against Quebec, many a night, lay down without food. In Captain Goodrich's company several became very weak from hunger, and at last Captain Dearborn gave them his pet dog. The soldiers carried the poor creature away and ate every part of his flesh, "not excepting his entrails." Two other dogs were eaten the same day.[3]

[1] Washington's Writings (Ford), vol. 5, p. 495.
[2] Washington at Morristown; his Writings (Ford), vol. 8, p. 186.
[3] Dearborn to Rev. W. Allen; note to J. Melvin's Journal, October 31, 1775 (New York, 1857), p. 14; (1864) p. 30.

By His EXCELLENCY

GEORGE WASHINGTON, Esquir

GENERAL and COMMANDER in CHIEF of the Forc
of the UNITED STATES of AMERICA.

BY Virtue of the Power and Direction to Me efpe-
cially given, I hereby enjoin and require all Perfons
refiding within feventy Miles of my Head Quarters to
threfh one Half of their Grain by the 1ft Day of February,
and the other Half by the 1ft Day of March next enfuing,
on Pain, in Cafe of Failure of having all that fhall remain in Sheaves after the Period above mentioned, feized
by the Commiffaries and Quarter-Mafters of the Army,
and paid for as Straw

GIVEN *under my Hand, at Head Quarters, near
the Valley Forge, in Philadelphia County, this* 20th
Day of December, 1777.

G. WASHINGTON.

By His Excellency's Command,

ROBERT H. HARRISON, Sec'y.

LANCASTER: PRINTED BY JOHN DUNLAP

Fac-simile (reduced) of a call for grain for the army at Valley Forge.
(Original owned by the Pennsylvania Historical Society.)

A story is told of two soldiers in another campaign who, being out of provisions, put a stone in their camp-kettle when a certain Colonel Winds was expected. The colonel soon stopped before their fire and inquired: "Well men, anything to eat?" "Not much," they replied.

"What have you in that kettle?"

"A stone, Colonel, for they say there is some strength in stones, if you can only get it out."

This guileless conversation had the desired effect, for the officer declared that they must have something better to eat.

In times of distress it was vexing to find that the wagon-drivers had ruined the pork by drawing out the brine to lighten the load;[1] or to see a clumsy fellow endeavoring to guide through the marshy road four or five horses attached to a wagon from which barrels of flour and other perishable provisions tumbled into the mud.[2] At Harlem Heights, soon after the battle of Long Island, the general saw about the camp large pieces of fine beef left untouched to putrefy in the sun.[3]

[1] Washington's Writings (Ford), vol. 4, p. 125.

[2] Dr. J. Campfield's Diary, p. 133.

[3] General orders, September 28, 1776.   American Archives V., vol. 2, col. 605.

[85]

The food was frequently poorly cooked from a
scarcity of wood for the fires, and the few trees
near a camp were the source of angry disputes.
" I thought," said Washington one day, "that
different regiments were upon the point of cutting each others' throats for a few standing lo-
custs near their encampments, to dress their
victuals with."[1] The quartermaster-general was
instructed to investigate complaints regarding
food and to punish careless cooks and bakers.[2] In
Wayne's command each regiment or corps had
an officer appointed weekly whose duty it was to
visit the kitchen or place for cooking in every
company, to see that the work was properly
done, and that meat was boiled, not fried. It
was recommended that flour be drawn from the
stores two days in each week, so that small
dumplings could be made for the soup.[3] When
the kitchen had no roof but the sky the soup
was often too thoroughly permeated with burnt
leaves and dirt to be palatable.[4] Better cooking,
especially baking, became a pressing necessity;

[1] Washington's Writings (Ford), vol. 3, p. 195.

[2] Colonel William Henshaw's Orderly Book, p. 44.

[3] Orderly Book of the Northern Army at Ticonderoga, p.
126.

[4] Dr. A. Waldo's Diary, Historical Magazine, May, 1861,
p. 131.

finally all bakers were placed under a director, without whose license no baker could work for the army.[1]   A year later a company of bakers was authorized, to consist of seventy-five men and a director who was to receive $50 a month and three rations a day.[2]

The beef was poor all through the winter of 1777-78, so lean and thin that it became a matter of jest.   A butcher who wore white buttons on the knees of his breeches was seen bearing a quarter of beef into camp.

"There, Tom," cried a soldier, "is some more of our fat beef.   By my soul, I can see the butcher's breeches buttons through it."[3]   It is not strange that the doctor who records this conversation was fervently grateful for a good stomach that he might endure "fire-cake" and water for breakfast, with water and fire-cake for dinner. At evening the cry could be heard along the line of soldiers' huts at Valley Forge, "No meat, no meat."   That the men under these conditions still showed "a spirit of alacrity and contentment" was marvellous.   Were soldiers to have

[1] Journals of Congress, May 3, 1777.

[2] *Ibid.*, February 27, 1778.

[3] Dr. Waldo's Diary, Historical Magazine, May, 1861, p. 134.

plenty of food and rum, wrote Dr. Waldo, "I believe they would storm Tophet."[1]

The fare of the enemy was not always better than that of the Continental soldiers, if confidence may be placed in the remark of a diarist that biscuit taken from the British regulars were hard enough for flints.[2]

The question of a sufficient supply of good food was of the first importance, and was seemingly as little understood by politicians of the day, as was the effect of clothing on enlistments, or of enlistment for short periods on the success of a campaign. Washington estimated that 30,000 men would require for twelve months at least 200,000 barrels of flour and 40,000,000 pounds of meat.[3] To obtain these supplies each year was one of the great tasks imposed upon the Commander-in-chief, and had confidence in Washington not grown from year to year and made his appeals effective, the Revolutionary War must have failed. To prevent the entire dissolution of the small permanent force which was deemed necessary during the winter months

---

[1] Dr. Waldo's Diary, Historical Magazine, May, 1861, p. 130.

[2] Military Journals of Two Private Soldiers, p. 53.

[3] Washington's Writings (Ford), vol. 8, p. 225.

of inactivity, food had to be saved for the support of these men that should have been available to maintain the militia when called upon for important enterprises.[1]

The method adopted to obtain supplies was simple in theory; the amount of flour, meat, and other necessities to be procured was apportioned to the various colonies to be collected, transported, and deposited at such places within the respective colonies or States as the Commander-in-chief might from time to time designate.[2] The same lack of a central authority strong enough to use force, which made it next to impossible to collect clothing, draft men, raise money, or punish deserters, played havoc with the commissary department. But when Washington in his vigorous, earnest appeals stirred the people near at hand they never failed him. The crises were always safely passed, and the war went on to the end.

Next in value to good food may be placed clothing, upon which depended largely the health, degree of cleanliness, and soldierly pride of the army. Frequent wars throughout the colonies from the earliest times had fostered the

[1] Washington's Writings (Ford), vol. 9, p. 45.
[2] Sparks in Washington's Writings (1834), vol. 6, p. 482.

military spirit along the Atlantic coast line and the inland frontier towns. At the outbreak of the Revolution militia and independent companies were to be found in all the colonies, and styles of uniform were almost as numerous as company organizations. From the simple dress of the New England alarm-list companies to the elaborate costumes of the private corps in New York, Philadelphia, or Virginia was a long step; and thus it happened that the levies raised from time to time on short enlistments to reënforce the Continental army formed a motley gathering. In the ranks at the siege of Boston were men dressed as savages,[1] as backwoodsmen, and some with uniforms not unlike those of the British regulars.[2] The general hue of the ranks, however, not only in the campaign before Boston but through much the larger part of the war, was sombre, and can best be indicated by saying that the browns and greens predominated.[3] Congress seems to have recognized this in an order to the commissioners at the Court of France in 1777 to

[1] American Archives IV., vol. 3, col. 2.

[2] A little later confusion arose from the similarity of the cloaks of the Connecticut light horse to those of the enemy.—Waldo's Diary, Historical Magazine, June, 1861, p. 169.

[3] Historical Magazine, vol. 4, p. 353 (December, 1860); also Magazine of American History, vol. 1, p. 461.

Chamber of Supplies, Watertown, June 18, 1775.

GENTLEMEN,

THE Welfare of our Country again induces us to urge your exertions in sending to the Magazine in this place, what can be procured of the following Articles, Salt Pork, Beans, Peas, Vinegar and Blankets, the prizes whereof as well as the Carting shall be allowed according to the Custom of your Place which we desire you to certify—It is of the utmost Importance that the Army should be supplied agreeable to the Resolve of the Congress more especially with these Articles, the four first of which are necessary for the Subsistence as well as the Health of the Men, and the other for their Comfort—The occasion of the Deficiency in *Blankets* is mostly owing to a number of Men enlisted from Boston and other Towns which have been vacated, and they all must be procured immediately or our worthy Countrymen will suffer.—

As the Country affords every thing in plenty necessary to subsist the Army, and we cannot at present obtain many things but by your Assistance, we assure ourselves that you will act your parts as worthily as you have done and hope that the Event of all our exertions will be the Salvation of our Country.

To the Selectmen and Committee
of Correspondence for the Town
of Stoughton

DAVID CHEEVER, per Order of
Committee of Supplies.

PROSPECT HILL.	BUNKER' HILL
I. Seven Dollars a Month.	I. Three Pence a Day.
II. Fresh Provisions, and in Plenty.	II. Rotten Salt Pork.
III. Health.	III. The Scurvy.
IV. Freedom, Ease, Affluence and a good Farm.	IV. Slavery, Beggary and Want.

Handbill sent among the British troops on Bunker Hill.
(Original owned by the Massachusetts Historical Society.)

send uniforms of green, blue, and brown colors.[1] The popular "blue and buff" were not worn by the Continental rank and file from New England or the South, and the New York and New Jersey troops, for whom the combination was designated between 1779 and 1782 were, much of the time, destitute of cloth of the proper colors.

During the opening months of the Revolution the troops that had no distinctive uniform were, as far as possible, clothed as Washington suggested, in a hunting shirt (a long loose coat), and in long breeches to which were attached gaiters or small-clothes buttoned at the sides and held down by straps under the shoes. The gaiters or leggings were often made of tow cloth which had been steeped in a tan vat until it became the color of a dry leaf. This uniform was sometimes called the rifle dress.[2] There were ruffles of the same material around the neck and on the bottom of the coat, on the shoulders, at the elbows, and about the wrists. The hat was round and dark, with a broad brim turned up in three places, in one of which there was usually a

---

[1] Journals of Congress, February 5, 1777.

[2] Magazine of American History, vol. I, p. 60, p. 461 *et seq.*, a valuable review of the subject by Professor A. B. Gardner of West Point.

cockade of some color or a sprig of green. A white belt over the left shoulder held the cartouch-box. A black cloth or stock went about the neck, and the hair was bound in a cue at the back.[1]

This costume was, in the minds of the British, associated with a skilful marksman, and Washington in the summer of 1776 urged its importance in these words: "It is a dress which is justly supposed to carry no small terror to the enemy, who think every such person a complete marksman."[2] At Bunker Hill a rifleman, standing upon the earthworks, was noticed by an Englishman to have shot as many as twenty of Howe's officers before he fell,[3] and in the Saratoga campaign, Anburey, watching the effect of their fire, attributed to the Americans a love of killing.[4] The British had reason, therefore, to fear the rifleman's dress.

The Provincial Congress of Massachusetts resolved July 5, 1775, to provide 13,000 coats, faced with the material of the coat, without

[1] See also Uniforms of the Army of the United States from 1774 to 1889, pp. 1–3.

[2] Washington's Writings (Ford), vol. 4, p. 297. Orderly Book, July 24, 1776.

[3] Trevelyan's American Revolution, part 1, p. 328.

[4] Anburey's Travels, vol. 1, p. 331.

lapels, short and with small folds, each regiment to have its number on the pewter buttons.[1] The general orders from head-quarters at Cambridge, July 24, 1775, recommended Indian leggings instead of stockings, as Washington hoped to obtain from the Continental Congress a hunting shirt for each man.[2] Leggings were also warmer than stockings, more lasting, and could be had in uniform color.[3] Congress, on November 4, 1775, resolved to provide clothing for the army, to be paid for by stoppages out of the soldiers' wages. At the same time it was ordered that as much as possible the cloth be dyed brown, and the distinction in regiment be indicated by the color of the facing.[4] It will be noticed that there was little attempt to introduce bright colors, which were less serviceable and less easy to obtain.

[1] American Archives IV., vol. 2, col. 1486.

[2] *Ibid.*, vol. 3, col. 248.

[3] Colonel William Henshaw's Orderly Book, p. 65.

[4] Again, having in mind the necessity of providing " the soldiers of the United Colonies " with clothing and blankets, Congress resolved, June 19, 1776, to recommend to the colonial assemblies and conventions that they cause to be made for each soldier a suit of clothes, the waistcoat and breeches to be of deer leather if to be had on reasonable terms, a blanket, felt hat, two shirts, two pair of hose, and two pair of shoes.

In the campaign about New York in 1776 many soldiers had no uniforms, and these men were provided with hunting shirts.[1] In October, 1776, Congress voted to give annually to each soldier who would enlist for the war a suit of cloths, to consist that year of two linen hunting shirts, two pair of overalls, a leathern or woollen waistcoat with sleeves, one pair of breeches, a hat or leather cap, two shirts, two pair of hose, and two pair of shoes.[2]

Writing to Governor Trumbull in January, 1778, Washington gave his opinion on a serviceable form of clothing, and added a word as to the value of trousers, now so universally adopted: " I would recommend a garment of the pattern of the sailors for jacket. This sets close to the body, and by buttoning double over the breast adds much to the warmth of the soldier. There may be a small cape and cuff of a different color to distinguish the corps. . . . As the overall is much preferable to breeches, I would recommend as many of them as possible." [3] The differ-

[1] American Archives IV., vol. 6, col. 426.

[2] Journals of Congress, October 8, 1776.

[3] Washington's Writings (Ford), vol. 6, p. 288. In General Sullivan's expedition in 1779 against the Six Nations in Western New York and Pennsylvania each man wore a short

ence desirable in winter and in summer is shown in the following letter:

"In June should be given a waistcoat with sleeves, flannel, if to be had, two pair of linnen overalls, one shirt, a black stock of hair or leather, a small round hat bound and a pair of shoes. In January, a waistcoat to be worn over the former, close in the skirts and double breasted, resembling a sailor's—, to have a collar and cuff of a different color, in order to distinguish the regiment, a pair of breeches, woolen overalls, yarn stockings, shirt, woolen cap, and a blanket when really necessary. Watch coats ought if possible to be provided for sentinels."[1]

Trousers or overalls were more and more recognized as necessary, and Congress by a resolution of March 23, 1779, directed Washington to fix and prescribe a uniform for the soldiers, being governed by the supply, "woolen overalls for winter and linen for summer to be substituted for the breeches." The adoption of blue coats followed in the fall; for in general orders dated at Moore's house, October 2, 1779, the

rifle frock, a vest, trousers of tow, shoes, stockings, and carried a blanket and an extra shirt.—Nathan Davis's History, Historical Magazine, April, 1868, p. 204.

[1] Washington's Writings (Ford), vol. 6, p. 330.

Commander ordered that the coats of the infantry be blue with white linings and buttons. The New England troops were to be distinguished by white facings, those of New York and New Jersey by buff facings, those of Pennsylvania, Delaware, Maryland, and Virginia by facings of red, and the troops of the Carolinas and Georgia by blue, with buttonholes edged with white tape or lace. The artillery coats were to be faced and lined with scarlet; they were to be edged with tape, as well as the buttonholes, and the buttons and hatbands were to be of yellow. Finally, the light dragoons or cavalry were to be distinguished by blue coats, with white facing, linings, and buttons.

It will be noticed that "blue and buff" had no standing in eleven of the thirteen States, although blue now became the military color of the United States.[1]

Signs of merit, common to all parts of the country, were adopted toward the close of the war. In August, 1782, Washington directed that a non-commissioned officer or a private who had served honorably for more than three uninterrupted years should be permitted to wear upon the left sleeve of the uniform coats a narrow angular piece of cloth of the color of the regi-

[1] Magazine of American History, vol. 1, p. 477.

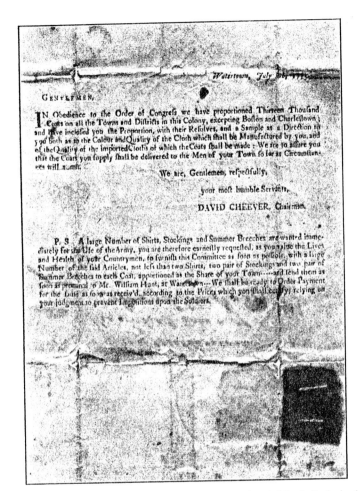

Watertown, July [...]

GENTLEMEN,

IN Obedience to the Order of Congress we have proportioned Thirteen Thousand Coats on all the Towns and Districts in this Colony, excepting Boston and Charlestown; and have inclosed you the Proportion, with their Resolves, and a Sample as a Direction to you both as to the Colour and Quality of the Cloth which shall be Manufactured by you, and of the Quality of the imported Cloths of which the Coats shall be made : We are to assure you that the Coats you supply shall be delivered to the Men of your Town so far as Circumstances will admit.

We are, Gentlemen, respectfully,

your most humble Servants,

DAVID CHEEVER, Chairman.

P. S. A large Number of Shirts, Stockings and Summer Breeches are wanted immediately for the Use of the Army, you are therefore earnestly requested, as you value the Lives and Health of your Countrymen, to furnish this Committee as soon as possible, with a large Number of the said Articles, not less than two Shirts, two pair of Stockings and two pair of Summer Breeches to each Coat, apportioned as the Share of your Town----and send them as soon as procured to Mr. William Hunt, at Watertown---We shall be ready to Order Payment for the same as soon as receiv'd, according to the Prices which you shall certify, relying on your judgment to prevent Impositions upon the Soldiers.

Call for coats, showing a sample of the fawn-colored felt-cloth desired. These broadsides are rarely found with the cloth still attached.

(Original owned by the Boston Public Library.)

mental facing.   For six years of service a parallel strip might be added.   Unusually meritorious action earned for the soldier a purple heart of silk or cloth edged with lace or binding, to be worn on the facing over the left breast.[1]

The uniforms of all the infantry and cavalry were later ordered to be blue, faced with red and lined with white—the buttons also to be white. This order, from the scarcity of scarlet cloth, did not prove effective until the war closed.[2]

The Revolution quickened the production of cloth (duck, Russia sheeting, tow-cloth, osnaburgs, ticklenburgs),[3] as it did that of shoes, gunpowder, and firearms.   Throughout the country towns women carded and spun the wool and flax which their husbands provided, and the cotton which came from the West Indies; then they themselves, or itinerant weavers, wove the flannel, linen, and corduroy.   In New England they usually received—but values are not easy to set down—five or six pence a skein of fifteen knots (about a yard and a half), and their day's work of from two to five skeins brought the value of

[1] Washington's Revolutionary Orders (Whiting), pp. 220–231.

[2] General Orders, Newburgh, December 6, 1782, February 24, March 3, 1783.

[3] Mentioned in a vote of Congress, July 19, 1775.

[97]

five or ten pounds of beef, or, to state it again, one or two good dinners at the tavern.[1] Prices in Virginia in 1776 varied greatly. John Harrower, a Scot, mentions in his diary a payment of five shillings a pound for spun cotton, to run eight yards per pound, or about seven pence a yard.[2] Weaving brought the same or a less amount. Many towns had mills for producing cloth, and the business of supplying the army grew rapidly. The campaign of 1775, however, was fought by men who had no clothing at hand suitable for very cold weather, and in many cases no blankets between their bodies and the ground.[3] The insufficient clothing was more serious in the expedition led by Montgomery in the autumn of 1775 to Montreal. His proclamation, promising every article of clothing requisite for the rigors of the climate, was intended to satisfy the men who were willing to go forward; it shows that they might expect blanket-coats, coats, waistcoats, breeches, one pair of stockings, two shirts, leggings, sacks, shoes, mittens, and a cap.[4] The

---

[1] Weeden's Economic and Social History, pp. 731, 789, 790.

[2] American Historical Review, October, 1900, p. 106 ; see also p. 107.

[3] Washington's Writings (Ford), vol. 3, pp. 142, 147.

[4] Lossing's Schuyler (1872), vol. 1, p. 464.

way to Canada might be said to have been paved with promises, and it proved to be a rough road.

In December, 1776, Washington referred to the distresses of his soldiers, " many of 'em being entirely naked and more so thinly clad as to be unfit for service." [1] The hardships of the year before had dampened the enthusiasm of the farmers, and enlistments fell off. The men had ragged shirts and many marched with their feet bare ; [2] a few days of active service resulted in sickness for want of proper covering at night and lameness for lack of shoes. Many deserted, impelled by indignation at what was believed to be the bad faith and indifference of the Colonial Assemblies. Colonel Angell, of Rhode Island, writing from Peekskill in August, 1777, to the governor of his State, declared that the condition of his regiment was so scandalous that the members of the other corps and people in the villages along the line of march called his men " the Ragged, Lousey, Naked regiment." [3]

These troubles reached their worst form in the winter at Valley Forge in 1777–78 and in

[1] Washington's Writings (Ford), vol. 5, p. 103.
[2] *Ibid.*, vol. 5, p. 151.
[3] I. Angell's Diary (Field), p. xii.

[99]

the summer which followed. The *New York Gazette* at this time reported humorously that Congress was *not* prevented from making more paper dollars by scarcity of rags, for " independent of the large supply expected from Washington's army as soon as they can be spared, we have reason to believe the country in general never abounded more in that article."[1] The dress of the soldiers was a favorite subject for jest, in one form or another, among the British. A poem addressed to Washington, who had issued a proclamation to the people calling upon them to fatten their cattle for his army, has the lines:

> And for the beef—there needs no puff about it;
> In short, they must content themselves without it,
> Not that we mean to have them starved—why, marry,
> The live-stock in abundance, which they carry
> Upon their backs, prevents all fear of that![2]

Upward of 2,000 men were unfit for service in November, 1777; in December there were 2,898 men in camp unfit for duty, many with no shoes and some without shirts. Many were confined

[1] New York Gazette, February 23, 1778. In F. Moore's Diary, vol. 2, p. 16.
[2] Rivington's Royal Gazette, January 2, 1779. In Moore's Diary, vol. 2, p. 118.

to hospitals and farm-houses with feet too sore to bear unprotected the winter snows.[1] When the trampled mud froze suddenly the rough ridges were like knives, and although men cut up their blankets and bound the strips about their feet the flesh was soon as unprotected as before.[2] Still others, in their huts, sat by the fire through the night and dozed, unwilling to lie far enough from the coals to sleep.[3] A fourth or fifth of the army passed the summer of 1778 about White Plains without shoes, and many with tattered shirts and breeches.[4] The winter of 1779–80 was endured by many without suitable covering at night,[5] and it is not strange that the young men in the country towns demanded exorbitant bounty money when asked to enlist in the following spring. If the Continental Congress could have offered good clothing and sufficient food soldiers might have been found for little or no bounty.

A vivid picture of Virginia troops is given by Thomas Anburey in his untrustworthy but read-

[1] Washington, December 29, 1777. In his Writings (Ford), vol. 6, p. 267.

[2] John Shreve's Personal Narrative. Magazine of American History, September, 1879, p. 568.

[3] Washington's Writings (Ford), vol. 6, p. 260.

[4] *Ibid.*, vol. 8, p. 333.   [5] *Ibid.*, vol. 7, p. 137.

able book of travels. The writer claims that the
colonel was proud of their appearance, and went
about with two troopers before and two behind
him, bearing drawn swords. Anburey writes:

"As to those troops of [Colonel Bland's Vir-
ginia] regiment with Washington's army, I cannot say any thing, but the two that the colonel
has with him here, for the purposes of expresses
and attendance, are the most curious figures you
ever saw; some, like Prince Prettyman, with one
boot, some hoseless, with their feet peeping out
of their shoes; others with breeches that put de-
cency to the blush; some in short jackets, some
in long coats, but all have fine dragoon caps, and
long swords slung round them, some with hol-
sters, some without, but gadamercy pistols, for
they have not a brace and a half among them,
but they are tolerably well mounted."[1]

While considering the lack of clothing, Washington wrote to General Lincoln: "What makes
the matter more mortifying is that we have, I am
positively assured Ten thousand compleat suits
ready in France & laying there because our public agents cannot agree whose business it is to
ship them—a quantity has also lain in the West
Indies for more than eighteen months, owing

[1] Anburey's Travels, vol. 2, p. 320.

probably to some such cause."[1] The effect of
this kind of official inaction upon the private
may be illustrated by an old soldier's experience
which he described to the historian of the First
New Hampshire Regiment. This man had, at
the time of these troubles, a furlough to visit his
home ; but the journey was a long one. Before
he could start he was obliged to spend two days
in cutting up his blanket to make for himself
breeches and a pair of moccasins.[2]

Two months before the siege of · Yorktown
began, the men were so destitute of clothing
that the French troops, encamped near by, made
jokes on the nudity of the Continentals ; yet, such
was their loyalty to the cause of the Colonies that,
when two ships from Spain arrived with supplies, and some of the coats were found to be
red in color like those worn by the British, the
Americans, ill-clad as they were, refused to wear
them.[3] A humorous view of the veterans was
taken by the " Peaceable man," as he styled
himself, when he " ventured to prophesy .   .   .
that if the war is continued through the winter,

[1] Washington's Writings (Ford), vol. 9, p. 51.

[2] Kidder's First New Hampshire Regiment, p. 72.

[3] Chevalier de la Luzerne, in J. Durand's New Materials, p.
250.

the British troops will be scared at the sight of our men, for as they never fought with naked men, the novelty of it will terrify them." [1] Times changed, however, and the winter of 1782–83 was passed at Newburgh in comfort; the men were better fed, well clothed, and sheltered. [2]

Ragged uniforms and poor food for a long time not only discouraged enlistments, but injured the efficiency of the men in the service. Soldiers grumbled, and if they did not come to open mutiny, they grew careless about their appearance and negligent in their habits. " Our men," Washington wrote in the orders of the day for January 1, 1776, " are brave and good ; men who, with pleasure it is observed, are addicted to fewer vices than are commonly found in armies. . . . If a soldier cannot be induced to take pride in his person he will soon become a Sloven, and indifferent to everything else. Whilst we have men, therefore, who in every respect are superior to mercenary troops, that are fighting for *two pence* or *three pence* a day, why cannot we in appearance also be superior to them, when we fight for Life, Liberty, Property and our Country ? "

[1] M. Morris's Private Journal, p. 16.
[2] Washington's Writings (Ford), vol. 10, p. 153.

IV

Firelock and Powder

ALTHOUGH guns were far more generally used at the outbreak of the Revolution than they are to-day, a serious problem in each campaign was to provide firearms for the troops. Each farmer in 1775 had his trusted flintlock, made usually by the hand of a village gunsmith.[1] With the disappearance of village artisans much of the charm and prosperity of rural towns has taken flight. The little shop of the cordwainer, or shoemaker, no longer resounds to the merry tapping of the pegs or the creaking of the waxed threads in his hands ; the

[1] The warlike stores in Massachusetts, and what is now Maine, reported April 14, 1775, aggregated :

Fire-arms	21,549
Pounds of powder	17,444
Pounds of lead balls	22,191
Number of flints	144,699
Number of bayonets	10,108
Number of pouches	11,979

(Journals of Each Provincial Congress, edited by Lincoln, p. 756.)

cooper and the broom-maker are so rare that few of the present generation have seen the one crowding his staves into place and the other shaping the broom-corn about the handle. The itinerant weaver, too, has passed away, and the miller no longer grinds the coarse flour, corn-meal, and buckwheat which delighted the children of a by-gone age. Who of us, looking through the advertising pages of a popular magazine, will feel any sentiment for the factories and mills pictured there—those unlovely successors of the vine-covered shops of the cordwainer, the cooper, the gunsmith?

To polish the barrel of a gun with buckskin and to keep a gloss on the stock by frequent use of oil and wax required more time than the average soldier could or perhaps would give;[1] so that during the war many of the firelocks soon wore out from exposure to the weather; some were lost in difficult marches, and others becoming broken could not easily be repaired, since the parts were usually hand-made and a new part had to be fitted to its place. The Continental Congress, July 18, 1775, in recommending the formation of militia companies, suggested that

[1] Major Elliott's Orders; in Charleston Year Book, 1889, p. 247.

Flint-lock guns, wooden canteen, and welded bayonet which were used by privates during the Revolution. The barrel of the lower gun has been shortened.

(Originals owned by James E. Kelly.)

each soldier have a good musket that would carry an ounce ball, a bayonet, steel ramrod, worm, priming wire, and brush fitted thereto, a cutting-sword or tomahawk, a cartridge-box to contain twenty-three rounds of cartridges, twelve flints, and a knapsack. The barrel was to be three and a half feet long. In time Congress established a Continental gun-factory at Lancaster, Penn., and a gun-lock factory at Trenton.[1]

When the militia soldier provided his own firelock his contribution to the cause was considerable for those days. In Massachusetts a gun and bayonet were estimated by the Provincial Congress to be worth £2;[2] in Pennsylvania in 1776 a gun brought about the same sum. In Virginia in 1778 a gun appears to have been worth from £3 to £5, and a rifle a pound or two more; a drum was valued at half as much. At this time £5 would buy about fifteen cords of wood, pay a laborer for two weeks' work, or purchase some fifty bushels of coal.[3]

The flintlock, or firelock as it was commonly called, was an effective weapon when supple-

[1] Journals of Congress, May 23, 1776.
[2] Journals, October 25, 1774.
[3] Virginia Historical Magazine, January, 1899, pp. 280–283.

mented by earthworks. At Bunker Hill, after two splendid but ineffective advances against the Americans in their hastily formed defences, General Howe saw that the bayonet was his last resource to silence their destructive fire. At Long Island the British used the bayonet with deadly effect, by receiving the fire of Washington's men and charging before they could reload.[1] Therein lay the weakness of the firelock, for the manner of loading was clumsy and slow. The end of the cartridge—a paper case filled with ball and powder—was bitten off, and a little powder was sprinkled on the pan;[2] the remainder of the contents was then dropped into the muzzle of the barrel and held in by ramming down the cartridge-case like a wad. The powder in the flash-pan, ignited by sparks from the contact of a flint with the "battery" (a piece of steel), communicated through a hole with the charge in the barrel. From this description it will be evident that the manual of exercise called for movements more intricate in loading and reload-

[1] Lord Percy's Letter; in Boston Public Library Bulletin, January, 1892, p. 325. A century before this it was part of a musketeer's training to draw his sword when hard pressed instead of attempting to reload.

[2] Sometimes "priming powder," of better quality, was used.

ing than were required later when the percussion-
lock came into use.

Until the introduction of Baron Steuben's plan
in 1779 the form of exercise in the regiments
was influenced by the previous training of the
colonels in English, French, or German methods.[1] The English systems in use in the Colonies before the war naturally had the greatest
vogue. In 1757 the Militia Bill was passed in
England to provide 32,000 men for home defence, so that the regular army could be employed abroad. As the new levies were to exercise but one day a week a simple form of
discipline was desirable; and that devised for
the county of Norfolk became so successful for
drilling militia that it was known widely as the
Norfolk Discipline. This plan was in favor in
New England as early as 1768, when an abstract
was published at Boston; and Timothy Pickering's simplification of the Norfolk was much used
at the North early in the war. Colonel Bland's
Treatise, published first in 1727, was more or less
in use in the South; a copy had been in Washington's library for many years.

The Massachusetts Provincial Congress, however, had in 1774 adopted the British army man-

[1] Steuben's Memorial in Kapp's Life (1859), p. 127.

ual of 1764 (known as the "Sixty-fourth"),[1] which, at the time the New Haven edition appeared, was in general use in Connecticut, Rhode Island, and Massachusetts Bay.[2] The words of command and motions for priming, loading, and firing a flintlock may be of interest in this age of rapid-fire machine-guns. The explanations are not given in full, as they are very detailed, to obtain uniformity in company drill.

1. *Poise your Firelocks!* - - - - - - 2 motions
> 1. (Lock outward, firelock perpendicular.)
> 2. (Left hand just above the lock and of an equal height with the eyes.)

2. *Cock your Firelocks!* - - - - - - 2 motions

3. *Present!* - - - - - - - - - - 1 motion
> 1. (Six inches to rear with right foot. Butt-end to shoulder.)

[1] Washington's own copies of Pickering and the Norfolk show no signs of wear; of the "Sixty-fourth" he had six copies, but the one in his library is fresh. His copy of the later work by Steuben bears annotations in MS. (probably his own), some of which were incorporated into succeeding editions. Sabin says that copies of Pickering's Easy Plan show much wear. It was adopted by Massachusetts in 1776. See Catalogue of Washington Collection in Boston Athenæum, pp. 135, 163. For an opinion of the Norfolk Discipline see the Monthly Review, vol. 21 (London, 1759), p. 340.

[2] Sabin's Dictionary, viii., 30771.

Plate taken from "Regulations for the Order and Dis

the Troops of the United States," by Baron de Steuben.

4. *Fire!* - - - - - - - - - - 1 motion

5. *Half-cock your Firelocks!* - - - - 1 motion

6. *Handle your Cartridge!* - - - - - 1 motion

   1. (Slap your Pouch, seize Car-
     tridge, bite the top well off.)

7. *Prime!* - - - - - - - - - - 1 motion

   1. (Shake the powder into the pan.)

8. *Shut your Pans!* - - - - - - - 2 motions

9. *Charge with Cartridge!* - - - - - 2 motions

   1. (Put the Cartridge into the
     muzzle, shaking the pow-
     der into the barrel.)
   2. (Hand on Rammer.)

10. *Draw your Rammers!* - - - - - - 2 motions

11. *Ram down your Cartridge!* - - - - 1 motion

12. *Return your Rammers!* - - - - - 1 motion

13. *Shoulder your Firelocks!* - - - - - 2 motions

   1. (Left hand under butt.)
   2. (Right hand thrown down at side.)

These actions were much the same in all the
manuals, although in the Norfolk they were begun chiefly from the shoulder, and not, as here,
from the " rest." Baron Steuben made his words
of command shorter and sharper. In the manœuvres greater divergence appears.

 At this time there were two serious objections
to the firelock: the soldier required so long to
load and fire it that a rapid advance of the enemy

close upon the discharge found him with no
weapon ready for defence, so that he was apt to
be overcome with panic; and the two qualities
of powder needed in the cartridge and the pan
for effective firing were difficult to obtain.
Franklin advocated the introduction of pikes;
and in a letter in 1776 gave strong reasons for
the use of bows and arrows, claiming that a man
could send four arrows for every bullet, that his
vision was not clouded by smoke, that his enemy
seeing the arrow (he could not see a bullet) had
his attention diverted from his duty, and when
struck he was less able to fight.[1]   It is interesting
to hear Colonel Thomson, a successful militia
officer of South Carolina, advocate the next year
for his regiment one hundred "complete riflemen with good horses and spears."[2]

The use of an old-time musket, which now
seems so cumbersome, led to frequent accidents.
In August, 1775, for example, a man forgot to
stop the end of his powder-horn; he flashed the
powder in the pan of his gun so near to the horn
that there was a conflagration which burned many

[1] Franklin to Charles Lee.   In his Works (Bigelow), vol. 6,
p. 2.

[2] Thomson to Rutledge, August 13, 1777; in Salley's
Orangeburg County, S. C., p. 452.

soldiers.[1]   Another man lowered his gun to re-
cock it, when there was a report and the gun
"kicked" him in the breast, producing instant
death.[2]   The force of these firelocks may be illustrated by an accident that happened in December, 1775; John M'Murtry, who was cleaning his
gun, put in the priming and pulled the trigger,
not knowing that it carried a load; the shot went
through a double partition of inch boards, through
one board of a berth, through the breast of a man
named Penn, and hit a chimney, leaving its mark
there.[3]

The scarcity of fire-arms made it necessary in
the autumn of 1775 for Washington to order
that no soldier was to carry away his arms if they
were fit for use; private property would be ap-
praised and purchased.[4]   In the following January he authorized colonels to buy guns which the
militia were willing to sell;[5] and yet a month
later 2,000 men in camp lacked arms.[6]   Colonel

[1] Rev. B. Boardman's Diary; in Massachusetts Historical
Society Proceedings, May, 1892, p. 404.

[2] Lieutenant I. Bangs's Journal, p. 55.

[3] A. Wright's Journal; in Historical Magazine, July, 1862,
p. 211.

[4] Washington's Writings (Ford), vol. 3, p. 233.

[5] Washington's Orderly Book, January 28, 1776.

[6] Washington's Writings (Ford), vol. 3, p. 406.

Ritzema's regiment in May possessed in all ninety-seven firelocks and seven bayonets.[1] In July of the critical summer of 1776 nearly one-fourth of the army had no arms,[2] and the New York convention ordered that each militia-man without arms should bring with him a shovel, spade, pick-axe, or a scythe straightened and made fast to a pole.[3]

One method of obtaining weapons was to disarm all disaffected persons,[4] and another means of increasing the supply was to purchase through local committees of safety the arms owned by men who for one reason or another were not likely to engage in active service. In Pennsylvania county committees of safety, by authority of the province assembly, appointed three collectors for each township. These men could call upon the nearest colonel of militia for aid or could bring before the committees any recalcitrants.[5]

Congress urged upon the Colonies the need of

[1] Washington's Writings (Ford), vol. 4, p. 65.

[2] C. F. Adams, in American Historical Review, vol. 1, p. 651.

[3] New York Convention Journal, August 10, 1776; Washington's Writings (Ford), vol. 4, p. 338.

[4] Journals of Congress, March 14, 1776.

[5] Minutes Bucks County Committee; in Pennsylvania Archives, 2d series, vol. 15, p. 359 *et seq.*

encouraging gunsmiths,[1] and the Colonies themselves imported large consignments of fire-arms
from Bordeaux in France.[2] Pliarne, Penet et
Cie., of Nantes, did a large export business and
claimed that they were able to send arms and
powder directly from the royal manufactories.[3]

Lead was to be had with less effort; that for
the campaign of 1776 was taken from the statue
of King George on the Bowling Green and from
the house-tops of New York;[4] and the amount
needed for the operations of 1777 came from the

[1] Journals of Congress, November 4, 1775.

[2] American Archives V., vol. 3, col. 1065.

[3] *Ibid.*, vol. 2, col. 1147.

[4] Washington to the President of Congress, July 3, 1776.

The following note is from the Journal of Lieutenant Isaac
Bangs (p. 57):

[July 10th, 1776.] Last Night the Statue on the Bowling
Green representing George Ghwelph, alias George Rex . . .
was pulled down by the Populace. In it were 4000 Pounds of
Lead. . . . The Lead, we hear, is to be run up into Mus-
quet Balls for the use of the Yankies, when it is hoped that the
Emanations of the Leaden George will make as deep impressions
in the Bodies of some of his red Coated & Torie Subjects, &
that they will do the same execution in poisoning & destroying
them, as the superabundant Emanations of the Folly & pretended
Goodness of the real George have made upon their Minds,
which have effectually poisoned & destroyed their Souls, that
they are not worthy to be ranked with any Beings who have any
Pretensions to the Principles of Virtue & Justice.

leaden spouts and window-weights of Philadelphia.[1] As the bore of the muskets differed in size the bullet-moulds were often of various sizes, and were joined together so that a soldier could make balls to fit any firelock. The running of balls—running the lead into the moulds—was a frequent duty in camp; it was noted one day by David How in his diary that he went to Prospect Hill after he had done his "steant running ball." [2] A quarter of a pound of buck-shot[3] or a pound of lead to be " cast into ball to suit the bore " was a proper allowance for a man.[4] In Stark's regiment each man on the day of Bunker Hill fight had a flint in his gun, and was served a gill-cup full of powder and fifteen balls for his cartridges.[5]

Powder was the crying need through much of the war. As early as 1774, the Provincial Congress of Massachusetts made an effort to provide powder; in December, Connecticut sought to obtain more powder, and Mr. Shaw, a New Lon-

[1] American Archives V., vol. 1, col. 366 ; see also Journals of Congress, July 31, 1775. There was also a good lead mine in Virginia.

[2] D. How's Diary, pp. 5, 30.

[3] A. Lewis's Orderly Book, April 19, 1776.

[4] Orderly Book of the Northern Army at Ticonderoga (1859), p. 24.

[5] Quoted in Trevelyan's American Revolution, pt. 1, p. 331.

don ship-owner, offered a swift vessel to go to the West Indies for this purpose.[1] " To maintain a post within musket-shot of the enemy for six months together," said Washington, " without [powder],[2] and at the same time to disband one army [*i.e.*, of 1775] and recruit another within that distance of twenty-odd British regiments, is more, probably, than ever was attempted." [3] Every effort was made to purchase powder, to encourage the manufacture of it, and to have the people save nitre and sulphur.[4] The Provincial Congress, two months before the battle of Lexington took place, resolved to appoint a committee to draw up directions " in an easy and familiar style " for the manufacture of saltpetre, these to be printed and sent to every town and district in the province at the public expense.[5] Furthermore, the Congress agreed to purchase all the saltpetre manufactured in the province for the next twelve months at a stated price. After the passage of this act a " simple countryman," it is

[1] Caulkins's New London, p. 508.

[2] The word was omitted lest the letter, if it fell into the hands of the enemy, should disclose Washington's precarious condition.

[3] Washington's Writings (Ford), vol. 3, p. 313.

[4] Weeden's Economic and Social History, vol. 2, p. 789.

[5] Journals Provincial Congress of Massachusetts, February 15, 1775.

said, brought into the House half a bushel of saltpetre which he had made, and promised that more could be made in eight months than the province had money to pay for. His method, the same as that described in the official Watertown pamphlet, is (in the language of a contemporary letter) " to take the earth from under old houses, Barns, &c., & put it lightly into a hogshead or Barrel; & then fill it with water, wch immediately forms a lie. This lie he then puts into an ashes leach that has all the goodness extracted before, this being only as a strainer. After it is run thro' w^{ch}, he boils the Lie so clarified to a certain Consistance, & then puts it to cool, when the saltpetre forms, & is immediately fit for use; & from every Bushel of earth he produces ¾ lb. saltpetre. On this information . . . the Act was suppressed for Amendment."[1]

The Congress at Philadelphia aided in the quest for powder by authorizing suspension of the non-importation agreement in the case of vessels bringing gunpowder or sulphur (with four times as much saltpetre), or brass fieldpieces, or muskets with bayonets, allowing them to carry out the same value, generously esti-

[1] Joseph Barrell to Joseph Green, November 3, 1775; in Boston in 1775 (Ford), p. 37.

mated, in produce from the Colonies.[1] Congress, on June 10, 1775, recommended to the several towns and districts in the Colonies that they collect all their saltpetre and sulphur, to be sent from the northern colonies to New York, from the central colonies to Philadelphia, and from those farther south to their committees and conventions to be manufactured into gunpowder.

The committee of safety in Philadelphia not only published the description of a process for making saltpetre, but called upon the local committee of each county to send two persons to learn the business at their works; these men when trained were, at the committee's expense, to travel from town to town for the purpose of instructing others in the art.[2]

The flint was characteristic of the gun of this period. The blunderbuss, a short gun with a large bore, clumsy and inaccurate of aim, had nearly passed out of use;[3] the old-time slow match which ignited the priming-powder had given way to the grooved wheel with serrated

[1] Journals of Congress, July 15, 1775.

[2] Minutes Bucks County Committee of Safety; in Pennsylvania Archives, 2d series, vol. 15, p. 354.

[3] Journals Provincial Congress of Massachusetts (Lincoln), p. 526.

edges, rotating against a flint, and this in turn passed out of use when the flint was fastened into the jaws of the cock and sprung against the steel hammer or cover-plate of the flash-pan. Each man when possible had at least two flints,[1] and also a wooden "driver" or "snapper," which was substituted for the flint at the time of exercise to prevent unnecessary wear of the stone. A good flint would fire sixty rounds before it had to be repaired, but the habit of snapping the lock was so prevalent that few flints did so much service.[2]

Flints were not easily obtained and workmen who could shape them were few. When "a vein of prodigious fine black flint stone" was discovered upon Mount Independence (near Ticonderoga) in 1776, the commanding officers of regiments were ordered to inquire if there were among their soldiers any old countrymen who understood the hammering of flints.[3]

[1] A. Lewis's Orderly Book, p. 29.

[2] Washington's Orderly Book, May 21, 1776; in his Writings (Ford), vol. 4, p. 100. General Greene, in his orders May 29, 1776, directed as a penalty for snapping locks two days and nights confinement on bread and water. (Long Island Historical Society Memoirs, vol. 3, pt. 2, p. 14.)

[3] Lieutenant E. Elmer's Journal; in New Jersey Historical Society Proceedings, vol. 3 (1849), p. 41.

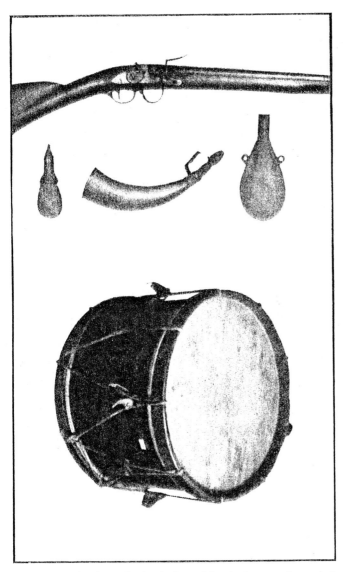

Musket, powder-horn, bullet-flask, and buck-shot pouch carried
in the Revolution (lent to the Bostonian Society by George B.
Dexter, Esq.).   Drum carried at the battle of Bunker Hill.

At the beginning of the war the farmers had their powder-horns, many of which bore designs and phrases expressing the sentiments of their owners. It was soon discovered that paper cylinders filled with powder and balls, and bound at either end with jack-thread, were more serviceable. They were ready for use in an emergency and in time of rain or snow; on the other hand, they could not be withdrawn except by firing the gun, and when powder was scarce the battalion or regimental guards (quarter-guards they were called) were instructed, it would seem, to charge their pieces with powder and "running" (loose-fitting?) balls that there might be no waste of ammunition.[1] The number of rounds carried by each man was less than the British regulars had at almost every period of the war, owing to the scarcity of cartridge-paper and powder. At the battle of Bunker Hill most of the men are said to have fired thirty rounds.[2] In the Quebec expedition Arnold's men had only five rounds apiece,[3] and during the winter of

[1] Massachusetts Historical Society Proceedings, October, 1876, p. 94; June, 1875, p. 90.

[2] Letter of Jesse Lukens, September, 1775; in Boston Public Library, Historical Manuscripts, No. 1, p. 25.

[3] American Historical Review, vol. 1, p. 296.

1775–76 Washington felt that he could not risk more than twelve or fifteen rounds at a time in the hands of the men.[1] Later on the Continental soldiers carried as many as twenty-five or forty rounds to be used against the sixty of the regulars.[2]

Given the firelock with powder and balls, there was still to be considered the man behind it; his skill and courage were worthy the attention of the Commander himself. In his book of orders, under date of June 29, 1776, Washington said to his soldiers :

" He [the General] recommends to them to load for their first fire with one musket ball and four or eight buck shot, according to the size and strength of their pieces; if the enemy is received with such a fire at not more than twenty or thirty yards distant, he has no doubt of their being repulsed."[3] When placed behind earthworks or a stone wall this had proved the best of devices. In the open field enough disciplined troops would survive such a fire to fall upon the raw recruits with fixed bayonets before they could, in their inexperience, load and deliver a

[1] Washington's Writings (Ford), vol. 3, p. 387.

[2] *Ibid.*, vol. 3, p. 426 ; vol. 4, p. 201 ; vol. 6, p. 71.

[3] *Ibid.*, vol. 4, p. 194.

second volley;[1] but the regulars were scarcely a
match for the militia when protected by earthworks.

Officers constantly advised the militia to hold
their fire until the enemy approached to within
a few yards of their defences; they gave orders
also to aim with care, for they knew that many
in the ranks were marksmen. When 500 volunteers were to be levied in the mountains of
Virginia in 1775, so many men came forward
that the commanding officer made his selection
by a trial of skill. A board one foot square
bearing a chalk outline of a nose was nailed to a
tree at a distance of 150 yards, or about the space
covered by fifteen to twenty houses in a modern
city block. Those who came nearest the mark
with a single bullet were to be enlisted. The
first forty or fifty men who shot cut the nose entirely out of the board.[2]

At Bunker Hill the American works were
silent until the British were within forty yards,
and where companies of grenadiers had stood,
three out of four, even nine out of ten in
some places, lay dead or wounded in the long

[1] See note No. 1, p. 108.
[2] John Harrower's Diary; in American Historical Review,
October, 1900, p. 100.

grass.[1]   A Scotchman living in Virginia said two months later that the slaughter of June 17th was to be attributed to the fact that the Americans "took sight" when they fired.

[1] Trevelyan's American Revolution, pt. 1, p. 328; Percy to his father, June 19, 1775 (MS. letters at Alnwick).

V

Officer and Private

IT is difficult to ascertain just what Washington thought of the private soldiers. When
by a disgraceful retreat, as once happened, he
was left in imminent danger of capture, he was
incensed at the cowardice of his men; when he
saw them enlist where they were offered the
largest bounty, he scorned their avarice; but
when they suffered and were patient, were tested
and proved loyal and courageous, he loved and
praised them. He put his trust in the native
rank and file, and chose for his bodyguard only
those born in America or those who were bound
to the land by the strongest ties of blood.[1] The
privates bore hardships such as, in his opinion,
would have broken the spirit of foreign soldiers.
In the spring of 1778 he wrote from Valley
Forge: "To see men, without clothes to cover
their nakedness, without blankets to lie on, without shoes by which their marches might be

[1] Historical Magazine, vol. 2, p. 131.

traced by the blood from their feet, and almost as often without provisions as with them, marching through the frost and snow, and at Christmas taking up their winter quarters within a day's march of the enemy without a house or hut to cover them, till they could be built, and submitting to it without a murmur, is a proof of patience and obedience which in my opinion can scarce be paralleled."[1] Colonel John Laurens, a young officer at head-quarters, shows in his letters a frank affection for the men whom he desired to command. " I would cherish," he said, " those dear, ragged Continentals, whose patience will be the admiration of future ages, and [I] glory in bleeding with them."[2] From the words of Washington and of Laurens it is reasonable to suppose that the rank and file were kindly remembered in the deliberations of those who formed the Commander's official family.

Washington knew the trials of the men who served under him; his kindly heart tempered the course of justice because he could measure the strength of their temptations. But officers were not always men of character—or, to use the old word, men of true quality—and the private, rea-

---

[1] Washington's Writings (Ford), vol. 6, p. 487.
[2] Army Correspondence of Colonel John Laurens, p. 136.

sonably patient under almost unheard-of privation and suffering, chafed beneath the yoke of
militarism. At the South the owner of a plan-
tation, having large opportunities for culture by
means of his great wealth, commanded respect,
and having many servants he grew to exercise
the voice of authority. At the North there was
none of this, and a distinction between officer and
man did not prevail in the rural militia of New
England.[1] This was due, in part at least, to the
levelling influence of small farms. The private's
company officers were not infrequently his inti-
mate friends or even his inferiors, men who had
devoted their time to the local militia organization and had become familiar with drill and tac-
tics while he, perhaps, was busy with other mat-
ters. The private could not understand why he
should salute such neighbors because they were
in camp, or why he should ask of them permission to go beyond the lines. When the men
gathered at the siege of Boston they were at first
allowed much liberty; a soldier, wishing to go
home for a few days, wrote a letter to a friend or
relative and asked him to come to camp as a substitute.[2] Before many weeks had passed the men

[1] See also Franklin's Works (Bigelow), vol. 4, p. 245.
[2] Green's Groton During the Revolution, p. 8.

noticed the increasing rigor of army discipline. Even a man of superior education, Rev. William Emerson, commented upon the "great distinction made between officers and soldiers," where everyone was made to know his place and keep in it, on pain of receiving thirty or forty lashes.[1]

Intelligent opinion was, on the whole, against the popular social philosophy of the day, when applied to army life. Joseph Reed, writing to his wife October 11, 1776, remarks: "Where the principles of democracy so universally prevail, where so great an equality and so thorough a levelling spirit predominates, either no discipline can be established, or he who attempts it must become odious and detestable, a position which no one will choose. You may form some notion of it when I tell you that yesterday morning a captain of horse, who attends the General from Connecticut, was seen shaving one of his men on the parade near the house."[2] The same impression was gained by James Wilkinson, who noticed in the camp at Boston but little distinction between colonel and private.[3] Graydon is

[1] Washington's Writings (Sparks), vol. 3, p. 491.
[2] Joseph Reed's Life and Correspondence (1847), vol. 1, p. 243 ; also American Archives V., vol. 2, col. 994.
[3] J. Wilkinson's Memoirs (1816), vol. 1, p. 16.

another witness; he recalls the story of Colonel Putnam, chief engineer of the army, who was seen with a large piece of meat in his hand. " What," said a friend, " carrying home your rations yourself, Colonel?" "Yes," he replied, " and I do it to set the officers a good example." And Graydon adds that if Putnam had seen any aristocratic tendencies in the army they must have been of very recent origin and due to southern contamination.

It was not at all uncommon for company or even regimental officers to give to their sons or younger brothers positions which were below commissioned rank.[1] But rank came to be more jealously guarded as time went on. In 1779, at a brigade court-martial, Captain Dexter, for behavior unbecoming the character of an officer and a gentleman in frequently associating with the wagon-master of the brigade, was sentenced to be discharged the service.[2] Earlier in the war Lieutenant Whitney, " for infamous conduct in degrading himself by voluntarily doing the duty of an orderly sergeant," was sentenced to be severely reprimanded.[3] Among a rural people at

[1] Graydon's Memoirs, p. 147.
[2] Colonel Israel Angell's Diary, p. 37, note.
[3] General Orders, Ticonderoga, October 3, 1776. In American Archives V., vol. 2, col. 1082.

The Private Soldier Under Washington

the North the lieutenant's act of kindness could
hardly have merited severity, except as it injured
discipline in other regiments. In the South more
was expected; Captain Barnard Elliott's Diary
has this entry:

"The Lieut. Col. cannot think the Major
could so far have overlooked the officers' command and authority as to order Shepherd (a private) to take a power only due to an officer;
he assures the regiment that in future if an officer
suffers his prerogative to be trampled upon which
he ought to support, he will be considered by
him as a man wanting in that essential which
constitutes the officer."[1] The practical results of
the doctrine of equality, when put in force, were
occasionally made evident by disorder and mutiny.[2]

While the lack of a proper difference in pay
for the officer and the private may have justified
in the mind of the private this attitude of equality, it could not have been the dominating influence among the troops from New England, if
it was among those from the middle and southern colonies. Washington calls it "one great

[1] Charleston Year Book, 1889, p. 256.
[2] Case cited by Colonel Weissenfels, July 6, 1776. In
American Archives V., vol. 1, col. 41.

[130]

source of familiarity." [1]   But the farmer of to-day
is more jealous of his right of familiarity with
the rich than with the poor, and more watchful
as his neighbor prospers.   To his reasoning a
larger income brings no enlarged prerogative in
social affairs.   Where social distinctions were
closely observed, as in the South, a marked difference in pay was more essential to the management of the rank and file.   But the difficulty
existed, and Washington wrote to the president
of Congress, September 24, 1776: " While those
men consider and treat him [an officer] as an
equal, and, in the character of an officer regard
him no more than a broomstick, being mixed
together as one common herd, no order nor discipline can prevail." [2]

What was the governing cause of this trouble?   Many have answered the question in
much the same words.   Captain John Chester, of
Connecticut, soon after the experience at Bunker Hill, commented upon the fear of all officers,
" from the Cap[t] General to a corporal," that
the people would brook no exercise of authority,
and added the significant words : " The most of
the companies of this Province [meaning Massa-

[1] Washington's Writings (Ford), vol. 3, p. 141.
[2] *Ibid.*, vol. 4, p. 443.

chusetts Bay] are commanded by a most Despicable set of officers."[1]

One explanation needs no proof to convince us of its truth. Where officers depended for their commissions upon their ability to raise companies or to persuade companies to serve under them, the test was of popularity and not of military skill. It proved impossible in Massachusetts for many men to play the double *rôle* of recruiting officer and disciplinarian before the same body of soldiers with success. Several officers who would have made excellent privates or officials in civil employment were turned out of the army in disgrace before the war was fairly begun.

If discipline depends upon those in command, what could be expected at Bunker Hill of a company whose captain ordered the men to march into battle, promising to " overtake them directly," and never appearing until the next day ?[2] " I have," said Washington, "already broke one Col°. and five Captains for Cowardice, or for drawing more Pay & Provisions than they had Men in their Companies."[3] General Lee and Captain Chester both speak of the ab-

[1] Boston in 1775 (Ford), p. 15.
[2] *Ibid.*, p. 14. [3] *Ibid.*, p. 29.

sence of officers from Bunker Hill, of lack of discipline, and of readiness to retreat among many companies of privates who had not so much as a corporal to command them.[1]

Men who had had little or no discipline at home needed a strong hand in camp, but a hand that they could respect. " As to the materials (I mean the private men)," wrote Charles Lee, " they are admirable—young, stout, healthy, zealous, and good humor'd and sober."[2] " But," to quote Joseph Hawley, " there is much more cause for fear that the officers will fail in a day of trial than the privates."[3] It was the officers who failed in their duty (if failure there was) at Bunker Hill;[4] they were the drill-masters on the green, but when the best stuff of the town was put under them and they were no longer merely drill-masters but leaders, they could not fill the measure. They were not always gentlemen, in so far as that term implies leadership in thought

[1] Boston in 1775 (Ford), pp. 14, 23.

[2] Lee to S. Deane, July 20, 1775. In Boston in 1775 (Ford), p. 22.

[3] Hawley to Washington. In Washington's Writings (Ford), vol. 3, p. 18.

[4] Washington, July 21, 1775. In *Ibid.*, vol. 3, p. 32. See also Dr. Belknap's opinion, in Massachusetts Historical Society Proceedings, June, 1875, p. 92.

and action. Some were petty, mercenary, overbearing, and themselves ill-trained to obey their official superiors. " These N. England men," said Lee, the professional soldier, " are so defective in materials for officers, that it must require time to make a real good army out of 'em." [1] The same sentiment was voiced in almost the same words by another famous general of the war, Nathanael Greene. " We want nothing," he said, " but good officers to constitute as good an army as ever marched into the field. Our men are much better than the officers." [2] It would not be well to condemn many for the failings which were too evident in a few; but the testimony of men like Lee and Greene suggests that when the private fell short in discipline and obedience, as frequently happened, he was not alone at fault.

The charge was once made that the rank and file served for money, while the liberties of Amer-

[1] Lee to R. Morris, quoted in Washington's Writings (Ford), vol. 3, p. 215. Ebenezer Huntington held a similar opinion ; see a letter dated June 29, 1775, in American Historical Review, July, 1900, p. 705. Graydon, in a rather unpleasant spirit, emphasizes the lack of men of the world and those of " decent breeding " among New England officers. (Memoirs, p. 157.)

[2] Washington's Writings (Ford), vol. 4, p. 441.

ica were preserved by the patriotism of officers.
In this connection a half-serious remark of Washington's, reported by an officer at Valley Forge,
seems applicable. " So many resignations of officers," said he, "that his Excellency expressed
fears of being left alone with the soldiers."[1] These
resignations, if we may believe Colonel Reed, were
sometimes prompted by cowardice. " I am sorry
to say," he writes in 1776, " too many officers from
all parts leave the army when danger approaches.
It is of the most ruinous consequences."[2] A fail-
ing among officers which was happily much less
common than mediocrity or even cowardice was
that of theft or embezzlement. The soldiery
were nearly helpless in the hands of those who
withheld the pay of their men from month to
month until mustered out of service or brought
to book by a court-martial.[3] The New Hampshire committee of safety—to mention a single
case—voted August 6, 1776, that Lieutenant
Gilman pay over to his men the coat - money
which he had the previous year received for

[1] Dr. A. Waldo's Diary ; in Historical Magazine, June,
1861, p. 169.

[2] American Archives V., vol. 2, col. 1036.

[3] *Ibid.*, vol. 2, col. 1128. The case of Captain Byers
(col. 1278) is typical.

them and had declined to deliver.[1] It would be unfair, perhaps, to assume that these malpractices were more evident in the revolutionary army than in any other army of volunteers; and it should be said that the self-sacrifice and heroism shown by officers all over the Colonies did much to put spirit into the rank and file.

An officer's ability to command carries with it a presumption that there is good discipline and obedience in the ranks. John Adams complained that soldiers loitered along the country roads and idled in the taverns.[2] In camp also, from time to time, there was a lack of discipline; soldiers were known to be on friendly terms with the enemy,[3] and careless sentries allowed their guns to be stolen while they were on duty.[4] The practice of hiring one's duties done by another did not sweeten the lot of the poorer soldier,[5] although this could hardly have been of frequent occurrence. Refusing to do duty, or threatening to leave the army,[6] were not uncom-

[1] American Archives V., vol. 1, col. 609.

[2] Washington's Writings (Ford), vol. 4, p. 438.

[3] *Ibid.*, vol. 3, p. 26. Also Army Correspondence of Colonel John Laurens, p. 70.

[4] Orderly Book of the Northern Army at Ticonderoga, p. 108.

[5] Essex Institute Collections, vol. 14, p. 63.

[6] Colonel William Henshaw's Orderly Book, p. 58.

mon breaches of discipline, brought about often by the unreasonable conduct of officers. Timothy Burnham, corporal, for keeping "Seymore" on sentry from six o'clock in the evening until seven the next morning, was reduced to the ranks.[1] Moses Pickett "for disobedience of orders and damning his officer" was sentenced to receive thirty lashes and afterward to be drummed out of the regiment.[2] The firing of guns in and about the camp was a constant annoyance that could not be stopped, and during the siege of Boston, British soldiers, hearing frequent reports followed by no casualties, came to ridicule American marksmanship.[3] Many of these acts of insubordination, however, are common to all armies.

In the winter of 1780–81, the mutiny of the Pennsylvania line, consisting at that time of six regiments, was one of the serious events of the war. The men were in huts near Morristown under the command of General Wayne; many of them had been engaged for the ambiguous term of "three years or the war," and now feared that they might be pressed to serve beyond

[1] Essex Institute Collections, vol. 14, p. 206.
[2] Colonel William Henshaw's Orderly Book, p. 81.
[3] *Ibid.*, p. 63.

the three-year period of their enlistment. At a
time when recruits were receiving large bounties
for short service, their own pay was already many
months in arrears, their food was poor and insufficient, and their ragged clothes were filthy. Reports were current that officers had used the men
cruelly, but these carried little or no weight.
The first day of the new year was celebrated with
an undue allowance of spirits, and soon the men
were ready to be stirred to rebellion by the picture of their sufferings artfully drawn by dema-
gogues. Between nine and ten o'clock of the
same evening the mutiny broke out under the
lead of Sergeant Williams, a deserter, poor, and
fond of drink. A number of officers were killed
or injured in a futile attempt to restore order, and
the men with six pieces of artillery set off for
Princeton. They marched with "an astonish-
ing regularity and discipline," allowing General
Wayne and two of his officers to accompany
them. On the second day Wayne asked for a
conference with one man chosen by the soldiery
from each regiment, hoping, as he said, "soon to
return to camp with all his brother soldiers who
took a little tour last evening";[1] but the rank
and file would not listen to his proposals, and the

[1] Stillé's Wayne, p. 252.

mutineers marched again on the 4th. Washington, meantime, apprised of events, was using every effort to bring about an agreement; he asked of the States a suit of clothes for each man and three months, pay. Clinton, of the British army, was not idle; he sent a message, addressed " To the person appointed by the Pennsylvania line to lead them in their present struggle for their liberty and rights," in which he offered to protect them, pardon any of their number for past offences, pay them what was due from Congress, and leave them free to give up military service if they wished. These were generous terms offered by the mother-country to her sons in rebellion. As they recalled their privations, and the uncertainty of their fate when they should again be in the power of Congress, they could hardly be expected to disappoint Clinton. Yet, as they put it, they preferred not " to turn Arnolds." [1] The Committee of Congress and Governor Reed, for the Council of Pennsylvania, offered terms which the mutineers accepted. The men who had enlisted indefinitely for three years or for the war were to be discharged unless they had voluntarily reënlisted, and where the orig-

[1] Wayne. Quoted in Washington's Writings (Ford), vol. 9, p. 97.

inal papers were not to be had the oath of the soldier was to be sufficient evidence. Certificates for the depreciation on their pay were to be given, and arrearages were to be made up as soon as possible. Clothing—a pair of shoes, overalls, and a shirt—was to be furnished as indicated in the proposals. Finally, no man was to be brought to trial or censured, but the past was to be buried in oblivion.[1] When these negotiations were completed the British spies were given up and executed. Many of the men, according to Washington's letter to Steuben, dated February 6, 1781, took the oath before the proper papers could be procured, and by perjury got out of the service.[2] The *New Jersey Gazette*, in a discussion of the revolt, remarks that the satisfactory conclusion " will teach General Clinton that, though he could bribe such a mean toad-eater as Arnold, it is not in his power to bribe an American soldier." [3] The unfortunate affair was not without other lessons, for men who could not be bribed

[1] Stillé's Wayne, p. 257.

[2] Washington's Writings (Ford), vol. 9, p. 123. See Hazard's Register of Pennsylvania, vol. 2 ; Marshall's Life of Washington (1805), vol. 4, p. 393 ; Remembrancer, vol. 11, p. 148.

[3] Gazette, January 17, 1781. In F. Moore's Diary, vol. 2, p. 374.

LIBERTY TREE

AN APPEAL TO GOD

Probably a Massa-
chusetts flag.

After an old print.

AN APPEAL TO HEAVEN

The flag of Massa-
chusetts.

A white ground with a pine
tree in the centre.

Flag carried by
the Bedford Militia
Company, at Con-
cord Bridge.

"It was originally designed in England in 1660-70, for the three county troops of
Middlesex, and became one of the accepted standards of the organized Militia
of the State, and as such it was used by the Bedford Company."

WILLIAM S. APPLETON, *Mass. Hist. Society.*

LIBERTY

Flag carried by the
American Army
through the South
at the beginning of the Revolution.

DONT TREAD ON ME

First naval flag.

A yellow flag with a rattle-
snake in the act of striking.

needed the best efforts of the commissary department in their behalf. The restless element wanted a firm hand, also, if the loyal majority was to remain obedient.

A few months later, at Yorktown, twelve plotters stepped out before the regiments and persuaded the men to refuse to march because the promises made to them had not been kept. Wayne then addressed them earnestly and called upon a platoon of soldiers to fire either upon him, who, with his officers, had been humiliated by the former disgrace, or upon the instigators of this fresh mutiny. At the word of command they presented and fired, killing six of the twelve leading rioters. One of the remaining six was badly maimed, and Wayne ordered a soldier to use his bayonet. This the man refused to do, claiming that the mutineer was his comrade. The general instantly drew his pistol, and would have shot the soldier had he refused longer to carry out the order. General Wayne then marched the regiments about the lifeless bodies, and ordered the five remaining mutineers to be hanged.[1]

In a recent work on the French army, Decle's

[1] Livingston to Colonel Webb. In Washington's Writings (Ford), vol. 9, p. 267.

"Trooper 3809," there is evidence of much friction between company officers and men. While something of the kind was suggested as the cause of the mutiny of the Pennsylvania line, this rumor never gained credence; the want of clothing and food was too evident a source of discontent.

The following order of General John Rutledge of South Carolina, in 1776, bears upon the relations between officers and their men, and it has the right spirit; it reads: "Any officer that shall strike a soldier at any time hereafter, whatsoever the provocation may be, such act of striking shall be imputed as an act of cowardice, save the Major and Adjutant [do it] and that tenderly and in the way of their particular duty."[1]

[1] Captain B. Elliott's Diary; in Charleston Year Book, 1889, p. 209.

VI

Camp Duties

THE soldier's life was not passed in idleness. Uniforms and arms required daily attention before the hour for parade, and the endless duties connected with cooking, obtaining fuel, and caring for the camp provided work for all. Day in camp began at sunrise with the beating of the reveille, or earlier when some important movement was to be executed. Not infrequently the exact moment of dawn was unknown and the tired men were called from their beds in the dark. Day was said, however, to have begun when a sentry could see clearly a thousand yards around him, " and not before." [1] To farmers' sons, unaccustomed to shave frequently, to put powder upon their hair, or to brush their clothes, a constant regard for personal appearance became at once oppressive. During the period of late sunrise the men were instructed to shave in the evening that they might be ready

[1] Colonel William Henshaw's Orderly Book, p. 53.

for parade in the morning;[1] and their canteens were to be filled at night whenever there was reason to expect an early departure from camp or an attack.[2]

In the opening years of the war many pickets, from ignorance of military life or from carelessness, brought trouble upon themselves; some went back to their quarters to get provisions, leaving their posts unprotected,[3] others sat down in comfort under trees, and, as just stated, were so negligent that their guns were stolen from their keeping.[4] Colonel Crafts at one time threatened to punish those who persisted in relieving themselves from duty without the presence of a corporal.[5] In September, 1775, the following description of military duty appears in a letter written by a Southern rifleman at Prospect Hill: "On Thursday at firing the morning Gun we were ordered to Plow'd Hill, where we lay all that day—I took my paper & Ink along as you once desired I would, but found so much to do beside writing, that you had only a few lines

---

[1] Orderly Book of the Northern Army at Ticonderoga, p. 26.
[2] Washington's Writings (Ford), vol. 4, p. 219.
[3] Colonel William Henshaw's Orderly Book, p. 47.
[4] A. Lewis's Orderly Book, p. 77.
[5] Essex Institute Collections, vol. 14, p. 64.

manufactured (in the face of 18 battering Cannon) ; . . . there was too much noise for writing & the Generals appearing in sight I tho't it not quite so decent a Posture of a SOLDIER, thrust my writing materials under an old Blanket, Shouldered my firelock, and strutted with all the parade of a careful Lad." [1]

As the autumn of 1775 wore on the men became accustomed to the routine and were more alert, although some failed to remember the proper password or countersign, since it was changed every night. A single sentinel demanded the countersign only, but the sentry next to the guard, upon hearing someone approach, demanded, "Who goes there?" and if many were in view he called to the sergeant of the guard, who ordered out his men under arms. When officers made the grand round the sergeant demanded the parole—a watchword not known to the guard—which he repeated to his captain. If the parole was given correctly he cried, "Grand round pass." [2] General Ward's selection of the parole and countersign was intended to impress

[1] Letter of Jesse Lukens; in Boston Public Library, Historical Manuscripts, No. 1, p. 26.

[2] Major Ennion Williams's Journal, Pennsylvania Archives, 2d series, vol. 15, p. 19.

wisdom upon the lonely sentinel, who was forced
to remember the words if he was unwilling to
accept their lesson. The parole *Industry* was
given with the countersign *Wealth*, *Neatness* with
Gentility, *Inoculation* with *Health*. In time of danger the parole *Look out* with the countersign
Sharp must have suggested to the sentinel the
path of duty.[1]

At Valley Forge there was a chain of sentinels
which surrounded the camp at the distance of a
mile; the men were relieved daily.[2] The following entry in Sergeant Wild's journal while
at Warwick, R. I., illustrates very well the per-
formance of guard duty. " At sundown," he
writes, " I carried my men to roll call. After the
rolls were called I mounted guard with sixteen
men under my command. I marched with my
men about 2 miles towards the Point, where I
left my guard. At 11 o'clk I sent a corporal
and four men out as a patrolling party, which
went down to the Point and all round the shore.
They discovered nothing remarkable. Came in
again about 1 o'clk, at which time I sent out an-

[1] Colonel I. Hutchinson's Orderly Book ; in Massachusetts
Historical Society Proceedings, October, 1878, p. 340 *et seq.*

[2] T. Blake's Journal, in Kidder's First New Hampshire
Regiment, p. 40.

other party, which went the rounds as before and came in about three o'clk; at which time I sent another party, which went the rounds as usual and came in between 4 & 5 o'clk, and then I sent another party, which patrolled till daylight and then came in with the other corporal and four men from the Point. I went to the commissary's, and got a gill of rum p^r man. After I gave it to them I dismissed them."[1]

Guard service in all kinds of weather, and sometimes in places of great danger, was not the least trying part of the soldier's routine, following, as it often did, days of great bodily exertion and fatigue. He who fell asleep while on duty was punished by twenty lashes on the bare back, or more if the enemy was near enough to make the crime a dangerous one.[2] The hardships which were endured called occasionally for a recommendation of clemency by a court-martial, as, for instance, in the case of George Cook, who was tried in 1777 for sleeping at his post. Cook had been ill of a fever for several days and unable to sleep; the fresh air of his lonely vigil brought relief, and he was found fast asleep, standing at

[1] E. Wild's Journal, in Massachusetts Historical Society Proceedings, October, 1890, p. 121.
[2] Orderly Book of the Northern Army at Ticonderoga, p. 56.

his place of duty.[1]   When a sentinel deserted to the enemy he became the subject of comment; "old countrymen," as the soldiers of foreign birth were called, never quite gained the confidence of the army, and if a man who was reported as "gone over to the enemy" was known to be an old countryman the fact was emphasized among the rank and file after the evening roll-call.[2]

Washington preferred "natives" for sentinels, and later he chose from them his body-guard.[3] He insisted that officers should place as sentinels at the outposts those whose characters were thoroughly known. "He therefore orders that for the future, no man shall be appointed to those important stations who is not a native of this country, or who has a wife or family in it, to whom he is known to be attached."[4]   Washington was driven to prefer Americans for officers, also, when the tide of adventurers from across the sea set in so strongly that it threatened to carry Congress with it and drive the native officers into retirement.   Lafayette, however, he contin-

[1] Putnam's General Orders, August 10, 1777 (p. 52).
[2] E. Wild's Journal; in Massachusetts Historical Society Proceedings, October, 1890, p. 96.
[3] Washington's Revolutionary Orders (Whiting), p. 35.
[4] Washington's Writings (Ford), vol. 3, p. 6.

ued to treat with an affection very like that of a father for his son.

Honor and kindness, while by no means unknown in war time, were not as common in the Revolution as the best military standards demand. Cases might be mentioned which did no credit to royalist or colonist. "About 8 o'clock," wrote John Clunes in March, 1779, "the Rebels sent in a Flagg of truse to us [the British], but Gen. Powell would not see [it] and ordered us to fire on them which we did and out of 5 killed 3."[1]

British treatment of the enemy's outposts was sometimes cruel and uncalled for. The following note by Lieutenant Eld, of the Coldstream Guards, describes an experience of his in New Jersey:

"I was sent forward with 60 Light Infantry to attack a rebel Picquet on the right of the main body of the rebels who were advantageously posted & fortified in a Church Yard at a place called Paramus. The Picq' was placed at the edge of a wood with a plain of half an mile in the rear,—I surprised the Picq' which instantly fled & the most famous chase over the plain ensued—we were in at the death of seven.—I had given orders that my Party should not fire

[1] Note to G. Pausch's Journal (1886), p. 151.

but use their Bayonets." [1]   After reading these
words it may be well to recall an incident which
is recorded in Simcoe's Journal, for it shows that
all the inhumanity was not confined to King
George's men :

" The rebels continually fired at night on the
centinels. . . . A figure was dressed up with
a blanket coat, and posted in the road by which
the enemy would probably advance, and fires resembling a piquet were placed at the customary
distance; at midnight the rebels arrived, and fired
twenty or thirty shot at the effigy. . . . The
next day an officer happening to come in with a
flag of truce, he was shown the figure and was
made sensible of the inhumanity of firing at a
sentinel when nothing farther was intended." [2]
This was not an isolated case, for David How's
Diary, under date of October 28, 1776, states that
riflemen fired at the sentries of the regulars while
the British army lay in sight, at or near White
Plains. [3]

The danger which a sentry encountered came
almost wholly from the sabre and the musket-

[1] Boston Public Library Bulletin, January, 1892, p. 314.

[2] J. G. Simcoe's Military Journal, p. 173.

[3] How's Diary, p. 35.   See also Heath's Memoirs (1798),
pp. 62, 63.

ball; but a curious exception recorded by the Rev. Benjamin Boardman should be noticed here. On Monday night, July 31, 1775, the enemy opened fire upon the Continentals from their works in Roxbury, and a cannon-ball came through the air so close to a sentinel that the man was set to whirling like a top. He soon fell to the ground, but was found to be only slightly injured.[1] A month earlier a soldier died from the "wind of a ball," as it was called.[2]

Camp life was not devoted wholly to drill or picket duty or cooking, although idleness was discouraged. Cutting wood, building fires, repairing huts, cleaning arms, waiting upon officers, tramping a road through the brush to facilitate the hauling of firewood,[3] serving in the "grass guard" to watch and protect the horses while feeding,[4] or making cartridges,[5] were use-

[1] Boardman's Diary, in Massachusetts Historical Society Proceedings, May, 1892, p. 400. See also Boston Public Library, Historical Manuscripts, No. 1, p. 28 ; the wind from a twenty-four-pounder knocked down a man and horse.

[2] John Trumbull's Autobiography, New York, 1841, p. 21.

[3] E. Wild's Journal, December 27, 1778 ; in Massachusetts Historical Society Proceedings, October, 1890.

[4] A. Lewis's Orderly Book, p. 10.

[5] Essex Institute Collections, vol. 14, p. 190 ; also Lewis's Orderly Book, p. 48.

ful services which kept the privates out of mischief. The construction of earthworks, building of whale-boats,[1] and other occupations incident to a campaign, filled the men's time while in more active service. In the expedition to Crown Point under Arnold, all hands were employed on occasion in necessary work; men were divided into squads, some to bake bread, some to go in search of game or to spend their time in fishing, others to cut timber or mount cannon.[2] In South Carolina seines were provided for the Continental troops that were detailed to fish.[3]

Temporary field-works of earth were not in favor in Europe a century and more ago; they were held to be unmilitary and to foster cowardice. But the defences thrown up at Bunker Hill in a night proved effective in checking the British advance; the firelock behind loose earth weighed heavily against disciplined bravery, and the lesson once learned, the Continentals entered more and more into the construction of

[1] Colonel Hutchinson's Orderly Book, p. 23.

[2] B. Arnold's Regimental Memorandum Book, June 14, 1775.

[3] Captain B. Elliott's Diary, in Charleston Year Book, 1889, p. 231.

such works.[1] The lines were first marked on the
ground in the angular forms so often shown in
illustrated histories covering this period. The
gabions (" stakes interwoven with twisted bundles of switches, like baskets without bottoms ")
were then set on the lines, three or four deep,
and earth dug up alongside was thrown in.
Fascines ("bundles of switches about six feet
long ") were then piled up on the outside and
inside, and were held in place by stakes, four
feet long, driven down through them ; more fascines were laid on top of the gabions, and the
whole was then covered with earth, and with
sod. In the space between the foot of the outer
slope and the ditch or fosse, which was a customary part of the works, wooden pickets were
frequently planted, as was the case at Bunker
Hill in October, 1775. Redoubts sometimes
had as additional works half-moon structures or
transes, as at Prospect Hill.[2] Farmers accustomed to handle the spade soon grew experienced
in this form of labor.

[1] C. F. Adams's Bunker Hill ; in American Historical
Review, vol. 1, pp. 411, 412.

[2] Major Ennion Williams's Journal ; in Pennsylvania Archives, 2d series, vol. 15, pp. 16–19. At White Plains General Heath made three serviceable redoubts of earth and corn-
stalks. (Memoirs, 1798, p. 82.)

Expert artisans were called upon to make paper for bank-notes,[1] print proclamations, and provide many articles in constant demand. These men were usually excused from all other duties, and found it to their advantage to exhibit their ability when called upon.[2] The dearth of skilled artisans in America is well illustrated by the petition presented to Congress in 1776, in which sundry paper-makers prayed that Nathan Sellers of Colonel Paschall's battalion might be ordered home "to make and prepare moulds, washers and utensils for carrying on the paper manufactory."[3] The "gunbarrel-maker," the saltpetre-maker, and he of the "nailer's business" were in such demand that they could hardly be spared for military service.[4] Forges had been set up all over the Colonies, giving employment to iron-workers and gunsmiths. The latter were not numerous, and a few of these accepted the bait or bribe of high wages in England, offered by leading royalists, and left the country.[5] Some of the soldiers were ordered to act as servants to their offi-

[1] Washington's Orderly Book kept at Valley Forge (Griffin), p. 5.

[2] A. Lewis's Orderly Book, p. 19.

[3] Journals of Congress, August 26, 1776.

[4] American Archives V., vol. 1, col. 1062.

[5] Weeden's Economic and Social History, vol. 2, p. 795.

cers; but as this kept many able-bodied men from active service and led to abuses, it was discontinued by general orders at Valley Forge in 1778.[1]

Knowledge of music was also in demand. In the Boston campaign the drums and fifes of each regiment were regularly instructed by the regimental drum-major and fife-major, and their music stirred the men as martial music does to-day.[2] When drums were not to be had, French horns were used.[3] In the campaign of 1779 against the Six Nations two men were cut down by the Indians' tomahawks; later Colonel Proctor ordered his musicians, in passing the spot, to play the touching air of Roslin Castle, "the soft and moving notes" of which cast a hush upon the regiment and awakened pity for their comrades.[4] The Pioneers March was another tune used at the time.[5] The memory. of one master of the drum should be kept green, for he helped to while away many tedious hours during the Northern campaign of 1776. Tibbals was his

[1] Washington's Revolutionary Orders (Whiting), p. 91.

[2] Colonel Hutchinson's Orderly Book; in Massachusetts Historical Society Proceedings, October, 1878, p. 347.

[3] Captain B. Elliott's Diary, in Charleston Year Book, 1889, p. 241.

[4] Rev. William Rogers's Journal, p. 35.

[5] A. Lewis's Orderly Book, p. 12.

name, and as the boatmen sang at their oars—
they were upon the lake—he would give one
touch upon the drum which seemed to bring
every voice into harmony.[1] The soldiers, half-
covered with water as they lay in the boats, forgot the loneliness and gloom of the darkening
night; the music lingered in each man's memory
long after the voices and drums were still. It is
probable that Yankee Doodle had little or no
vogue in the army, and the statement by Anburey that the lively air was "a favorite of fav-
orites . . . the lover's spell, the nurse's lullaby"
is open to serious question.[2] At funerals the im-
pressive tune Funeral Thoughts, with its drum-beat
at the end of each line, was sometimes played.[3]

Washington made use of the artisan in the
army whenever it was possible, but there were
many occasions when capable hands were able to
turn a penny after the soldier's day had closed.
Early in the war, barter and private labor pre-
vailed among the thrifty to a surprising degree;
men worked at their trades during the hours be-

[1] Rev. A. R. Robbins's Journal, pp. 18, 43.

[2] T. Anburey's Travels, vol. 2, p. 50. Thacher's Military Journal, p. 128.

[3] Rev. B. Boardman's Diary, in Massachusetts Historical Society Proceedings, May, 1892, p. 411.

tween the Retreat, which beat at sunset, and the Tattoo, which was sounded at eight or nine o'clock.[1] The makers of shoes, leather breeches, or caps earned money, and by their work aided to some extent the efforts of the Colonies to clothe the army. David How, a private at the siege of Boston, bought and sold cider, chestnuts, arms, and clothing. A few lines from his diary will show the busy life that a soldier might lead when not on duty :

25 *day* [January, 1776]. I Bought 7 Bushels of Chesnuts & give 4 pisterens per bushel.

30 We have Sold Nuts and Cyder Every Day this Weak.

31 I Bought 4 Bushels of Apels and gave 12s. pr Bushel for them.

22 [February]. PETER GAGE Staid Hear Last Night and I Bought 3 pare of Shoes of him @ 5/6 per pare. I Bought a pare of Stocking And give 5/4 for them. .

23 I Sold a pare of Shoes for 6/8.

26 I Sold my Cateridge box For 4/6 Lawfull money.

---

[1] At the same time British soldiers earned money by working for the inhabitants of Boston, although this was contrary to orders. (Diary of S. Kemble, Lieutenant-Colonel Sixtieth Foot ; in New York Historical Society Collections, 1883, p. 72.) Private work is still carried on where one might least expect to see it, by sailors on British men-of-war. (F. T. Bullen, in the Spectator, September 9, 1899.)

At the time he carried on this trading he was quartered in one of the buildings at Harvard College, and did his share of fatigue, made cartridges, ran ball, and even served his turn as cook for the company.[1]

A curious agreement, made between a soldier and a land-owner near camp, stipulated that the former was to clear a certain tract of land fit for mowing, and was to receive $100 paper currency, but if head-quarters moved before he had finished the work, he was to receive payment for what he had done.[2]

Among the many duties incident to army life the observance of Sunday as a day for religious teaching was not forgotten. Washington himself impressed upon the men under his command the value of Christian character, and his own example must have aided the chaplains in their difficult labors.

Public prayers were a part of the daily or Sunday routine, followed by the reading of orders, and usually the roll-call.[3] Washington's attitude toward religion in the army was unmistakably

[1] David How's Diary, p. 4 *et seq.*
[2] Elijah Fisher's Journal, p. 11.
[3] Rev. William Emerson, in Washington's Writings (Sparks), vol. 3, p. 491.

set forth when he said: " To the distinguished
character of a Patriot, it should be our highest
glory to add the more distinguished character of
a Christian." [1]   And Congress, ready to promote
the same ideals, voted September 11, 1777, to
import twenty thousand Bibles; it is curious to
notice that all the members from New England
were in favor of the measure, and all those from
the Southern States, except Georgia, were recorded as against it, although Lee of Virginia and
Laurens of South Carolina were with the North.

A chaplain, who, it is said, "prayed and sang
with the brigade," has described the preparation
made for services: " The music march up and
the drummers lay their drums in a very neat style
in two rows, one above the other; it always takes
five, and often the rows are very long; occasionally they make a platform for me to stand upon,
and raise their drums a number of tier." [2]   The
sermon on Sunday, usually at eleven, was often
of a practical nature; it referred to the hardships
and the duties of a soldier; it urged upon him
temperance and vigilance, cleanliness and honesty.
In many cases, as in those cited herewith, the minister altered the text to suit his need.   Rev. John

[1] Washington's Revolutionary Orders (Whiting), p. 75.
[2] Rev. A. R. Robbins's Journal, p. 37.

Gano, who was attached to Clinton's division of the expedition against the Six Nations in 1779, was asked to preach to the troops at Canajoharie, and was requested "to dwell a little more on politics" than he usually did. He preached from the words of Moses:

"Come, go thou with us, and we will do thee good; for he that seeketh my life, seeketh thy life, but with us thou shalt be in safeguard." [1]

Rev. Mr. Kirtland preached September 15, 1776, to the New Jersey troops at Fort Schuyler from the text, "He that is not with me is against me; and he that gathereth not with me, scattereth abroad." [2] Upon the 4th of July, Mr. Gano took for his text these words: "This day shall be a memorial unto you throughout your generations." [3] But these suggestive sermons did not always attract the men, and even when they were present discipline was not maintained as rigidly as would be the case to-day. To increase the audience a penalty was once imposed for absence from

[1] A practical adaptation from 1 Samuel xxii. 23.

[2] Lieutenant E. Elmer's Journal; New Jersey Historical Society Proceedings, vol. 3 (1849), p. 25. The reading in Matthew xii. 30, "with me," was changed by the minister to "for me," perhaps to strengthen his text.

[3] From Exodus xii. 14.

[160]

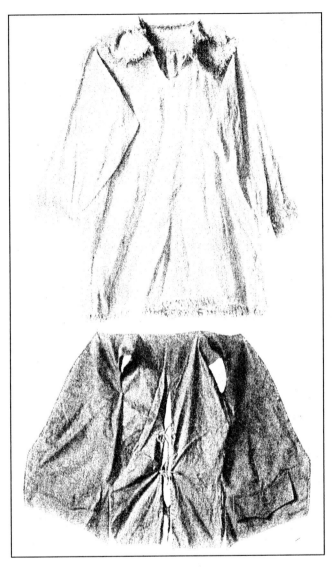

Hunting shirt (made from a model of the Revolutionary period) of home-spun linen. Vest made from a model of that period showing lacing in back instead of a buckle.

(Originals owned by James E. Kelly.)

worship : a few hours spent in digging out stumps in a New York woodland proved effective.[1] It should be said in defence of the men that the preaching was not always worth a hearing. Mr. Bliss, said a fellow clergyman, preached at Cambridge August 20, 1775, "from those words in Deut. 23, 9–14, and had he have digested his subject might have done well, but attempting to extemporize, *it was as it was.*"[2] The critic himself, however, rather outdid Mr. Bliss on the following Sunday, when, as he records, he preached the entire day; but perhaps he had relays of listeners, and not one weary throng, as might be inferred.[3]

Rev. Mr. Gano was a serviceable preacher. When he was informed that many of the soldiers before whom he was to preach on a certain Sunday were six and nine months men, whose departure from the army would be unfortunate, he told his listeners that "he could aver of the truth that our Lord and Saviour approved of all those who had engaged in His service for the whole warfare." The rank and file were much amused, and those

[1] Rev. John Gano's Biographical Memoirs (New York, 1806); also Historical Magazine, vol. 5, p. 332.

[2] Rev. B. Boardman's Diary; Massachusetts Historical Society Proceedings, May, 1892, p. 403.

[3] *Ibid.*, p. 404.

[161]

who had "engaged for the whole war" forced many short-term men by their jesting to re-enlist.

But the laugh was not always on the ministers' side. During the winter at Valley Forge many parsons were at home, as the men were too poorly clad to stand in the cold and listen to preaching. Mr. Gano was away on leave; when he returned to camp he asked a soldier how his commander and the men had fared. The soldier replied gravely that they had suffered all winter without hearing the Word of God. Mr. Gano explained that it was their comfort he had had in mind.

"True," said the soldier, "but it would have been consoling to have had such a good man near us." Deeply touched, Mr. Gano told General van Cortlandt of his encounter. Van Cortlandt, a little later, asked to have the soldier pointed out to him, and was surprised to see the worst reprobate in the regiment.[1]

[1] P. van Cortlandt's Autobiography ; in Magazine of American History, May, 1878, p. 296.

VII
Camp Diversions

RUMORS of victory or defeat lent a pleasant excitement to the lives of the rank and file. A story of the patriot campaign in Canada was passed on, together with official dispatches, from one post-rider to another along the almost impassable river-routes of Maine, over the stony roads of Massachusetts and Connecticut, through the Tory settlements of New York, and so southward to the Congress at Philadelphia; the dispatches reached their destination unchanged except for a coating of grime and wet, but the verbal story grew with each retelling until the last post-rider had news to astonish those about the camp-fires. The official news was printed upon handbills, which were given out to the men.[1]

The effect of good tidings is shown in a somewhat famous scene. When the stores from the captured ship Nancy arrived in the camp near

[1] Washington's Writings (Ford), vol. 6, p. 65.

Boston, there were demonstrations of joy. The scene as pictured by Colonel Moylan is somewhat startling: "Old Put [General Putnam] was mounted on the mortar, with a bottle of rum in his hand, standing parson to christen, while godfather Mifflin gave it the name of Congress."[1]

Bands of prisoners of war and captive Tories, passing through the camp, awakened patriotic enthusiasm, which found expression in shouts from the men; and the coming of well-known or curious visitors—delegates from Congress, sent to inspect the army, or Indian chiefs and their followers—helped to while away the hours. The impression made by such events is illustrated in the record in a soldier's diary that "the King of the Ingans with five of his Nobles to attend him come to Head Quarters to Congrattulate with his exelency."[2]

For many years June 4th, the King's birthday, had been celebrated in America; and when the day was allowed to pass in camp with no festivity and no mirth, even the rebel in arms could not but notice this sorry end of a time-honored

---

[1] Quoted in The Military Journals of Two Private Soldiers, 1758–75, p. 83.

[2] David How's Diary, p. 12.

custom.[1]   When September 22d, the King's coronation day, was referred to as the King's " Damnation day," war had indeed come.[2]

The great day was the Fourth of July, commonly called the anniversary " of our Independency." Few diaries fail to mention with some detail the usual ceremonies of the occasion. The whole army was drawn up under arms at one o'clock, with detachments of artillery interspersed and thirteen pieces at the right. The celebration began with a discharge of thirteen shots for the States, followed by a running fire of musketry and cannon from right to left through the front ranks, and then from left to right through the second line, repeated three times. A speech sometimes followed, and then three cheers from the entire army.[3] Games and an extra allowance of rum closed the day. On the British prison-ships, where all the horrors of starvation, suffocation, and disease were rife, the day brought a speech or a feeble cheer.[4]

[1] Lieutenant Isaac Bangs's Journal, p. 39.

[2] Daniel McCurtin's Journal ; in T. Balch's Papers (1857), p. 17.

[3] Henry Dearborn's Journals, p. 18 ; Washington's Writings (Ford), vol. 7, p. 482 ; Feltman's Journal, p. 6 ; T. Blake's Journal, p. 43.

[4] Martyrs of the Revolution in British Prison-ships, p. 20.

Another favorite anniversary was that of the day of Burgoyne's surrender, which was celebrated by the firing of cannon, the throwing of sky-rockets into the air ("skilokets in the are"), and much merrymaking.[1] When the welcome news was received that France had declared for the United States, the delighted troops cheered for the King of France, the "Friendly powers" of Europe, and the thirteen States; every Continental soldier under arrest in Washington's army was set at liberty to enjoy the day.[2] On more than one occasion a soldier under sentence of death profited by the news that the French King had shown his friendship for the Colonies or that a distant battle had been won.

But the successes of the British bore hard upon the men in the patriot army; and sometimes even those in captivity were made to know that their captors had won a victory. Major Griffith Williams, in command of the detachment of Royal Artillery with Burgoyne, ordered that the American prisoners be drawn up in the rear of the British lines, to hear the "feu de joye" given in honor of Burgoyne's victories. Some, it is said,

[1] Elijah Fisher's Journal, p. 10.

[2] *Ibid.*, p. 8 ; also T. Blake's Journal, in Kidder's First New Hampshire Regiment, p. 41.

were stung by the insult, while others threw up their caps with the British and were roughly handled by their more loyal comrades.[1]

The customary holidays were not forgotten; Christmas and Thanksgiving Day brought greater liberties and an extra allowance of liquor.[2] Even St. Patrick's Day produced a noticeable change in camp;[3] the Irishmen who had been born in America or had settled in the country before the war began were reënforced in some regiments by deserters from the British lines.[4] The widow Izard, a prominent lady in the South, honored the name of St. Patrick in 1782 by a gift of a gill of spirits to each soldier in General Greene's army. A little later the same army celebrated May Day with May-poles and festivities, although this was declared to be " something extraordinary," as indeed it must have been.[5]

Victories and anniversaries brought merriment

[1] Hadden's Journal, p. 102. Hadden did not approve of Major Williams's treatment of American prisoners.

[2] H. Dearborn's Journals, 1776–83, p. 25.

[3] Ebenezer Wild's Diary ; in Massachusetts Historical Society Proceedings, October, 1890, p. 133.

[4] Kemble's Journal (New York Historical Society Collections, 1883) mentions Irish deserters from both armies.

[5] W. McDowell's Journal ; in Pennsylvania Archives, 2d series, vol. 15, pp. 314, 321.

and noise, with their accompaniment of drinking and cursing. Congress occasionally showed an interest in these celebrations and sent the inevitable present of rum; thirty hogsheads were consumed by the gallant survivors of the battle of the Brandywine.[1]

But there were other forms of amusement in camp. The men played ball or cards, and now and then were allowed a " rifle frolic "—a contest in marksmanship in which the vanquished was bound to treat his more skilful adversary to liquor.[2] A form of relaxation not so clearly understood is mentioned by private Samuel Haws as " an old fudg fairyouwell my friends." [3] During the winter of 1775–76, which was bitterly cold at the north, men enjoyed skating on the rivers and ponds ;[4] and in summer they bathed whenever it was possible.[5] They sometimes were able to get away into the country to fish, hunt, and to gather nuts,[6] but these privileges were more often granted to officers.[7]

[1] Journals of Congress, September 12, 1777.
[2] Military Journals of Two Private Soldiers, p. 77.
[3] *Ibid.*, p. 80.   [4] *Ibid.*, p. 90.
[5] Colonel W. Henshaw's Orderly Book, p. 72.
[6] Military Journals of Two Private Soldiers, p. 77.
[7] A. Lewis's Orderly Book (Richmond, 1860), p. 65 ; also Feltman's Journal.

Company receipt for pay showing the ability of the private to write.
(Original owned by the Boston Public Library.)

Nothing so depressed the spirits of the soldiers as the inactive life of a camp far removed from the enemy. A spice of danger was always welcome. To train the raw recruits to be fearless under fire a trifling reward was offered for bringing to head-quarters each cannon-ball which was thrown from the enemy's batteries. It was found, however, that the younger men failed to gauge properly the force and weight of a ball that ricochetted slowly along the uneven ground; several soldiers in using their feet to bring a ball to a stop were knocked down or crippled. This plan had to be given up.[1] When the shells from Boston fell into the camp at Roxbury, shrieking like "a flock of geese," they did more, said an observer, "to exhilarate the spirits of our people than 200 gallons of our New England rum." Each shell as soon as it burst was surrounded by a throng of men, eager for mementoes.[2]

Funerals, someone has said, must be counted with amusements in a description of uneventful country life. The chastisement of wrong-doers may likewise fall into line with the diversions of

[1] John Trumbull's Autobiography (1841), p. 19.
[2] Jabez Fitch's Diary; in Massachusetts Historical Society Proceedings, May, 1894, p. 45.

camp-life, without great impropriety; for the curious modes of punishment in vogue at the time afforded some relaxation, if they did not convey the obvious lesson. The moral to be taken to heart by the onlookers was weakened by the frequent reprieve of the culprit; and this misfortune was only too well understood by the officers.[1]   One hundred lashes—the limit of corporal punishment allowed—made little impression upon the spirit of a sullen and wilful transgressor.[2]   To give a hundred lashes their proper value and importance, standing, as they did, for the penalty next to death itself, many serious

---

[1] The articles of war were approved by the Continental Congress June 30 and November 7, 1775.   Article LI. reads : That no persons shall be sentenced by a court-martial to suffer death, except in the cases expressly mentioned in the foregoing articles ; nor shall any punishment be inflicted at the discretion of a court-martial, other than degrading, cashiering, drumming out of the army, whipping not exceeding thirty-nine lashes, fine not exceeding two months' pay of the offender, imprisonment not exceeding one month.

The articles approved for the army September 20, 1776, directed in Section XVIII., Article 3, that corporal punishment should not exceed 100 lashes.

[2] One hundred lashes could be made very effective, as in the case of one Burris, who received fifty lashes a day for two successive days, and then was well washed with salt and water.— Washington's Revolutionary Orders, edited by Whiting, March 25, 1778.

crimes that needed severe treatment had to be met with inadequate punishment. The result as it worked out in practice was that the death penalty was too often imposed, and this led to reprieves. Another unfortunate outcome of the system was the invention of new punishments, more or less cruel or savage, when officers became exasperated by desertions and mutiny.[1]

A corporal and two privates were making their escape from the First Pennsylvania Regiment when they were overtaken and captured. After they had been secured a dispute arose; some of the captors wished to kill all three on the spot, without trial and without authority; others counselled delay. It was agreed finally to kill one of the three deserters immediately; the three luckless fellows drew lots and fate selected the corporal, whose head was at once cut off and placed upon a pole. This grewsome object was carried into camp by the surviving captives, to be placed over the camp gallows as a warning to all.[2]

[1] Washington's Writings (Ford), vol. 9, p. 128. The British army regulations of to-day do not permit more than twenty-five strokes at a time. See Wyndham's Queen's Service, pp. 243, 245.

[2] William Irvine to Wayne, July 10, 1779; in Philips's Historic Letters.

If there can be any excuse for such savagery it is to be found in the jeopardy of a great cause by desertions from an already inadequate army. Washington once wrote: "Our army is shamefully reduced by desertion, and except the people in the country can be forced to give information when deserters return to their old neighborhoods, we shall be obliged to detach one half the army to bring back the other." [1]

In the country about New York many of the inhabitants were from principle or interest trimmers in those uncertain times. Men when drafted were slow to respond to the call, and many, after enduring the hardships of camp-life for a time, returned home to aid a sick or impoverished household. They had perhaps begged in vain for an honorable discharge, telling, as others did throughout the Colonies, of little ones without food or firewood; [2] and when they appeared in town again the neighbors beheld the deserters with tolerance or with half-kindly eyes. In a letter written at Rhinebeck, September 16, 1776, John White said: "I suppose there are not less in this and Northeast Precinct than thirty [de-

[1] Washington's Writings (Ford), vol. 5, p. 211.
[2] American Historical Review, July, 1900, p. 721.

Receipt signed by the Ipswich minute-men who marched on the alarm
of April 19, 1775.

(Original in the Emmet collection in the Lenox Library, New York.)

serters], who keep in the woods, and are supported by their friends."[1]

Ebenezer Wild in his Revolutionary journal refers frequently to punishments, and it is evident that they interested him by their variety and terrible reality. Upon one occasion the culprits marched to the place of execution to the strains of the " Dead March," each one with his coffin borne before him. The brigade was then paraded, with the guilty men in front where they could be seen; after this their death sentences were read in a loud voice. Their graves were dug, the coffins were laid beside them, and each man was commanded to kneel beside his future resting-place in mother earth while the executioners received their orders to load, take aim and——

At this critical moment a messenger appeared with a reprieve which was read aloud.[2] This last all-important act in the series was omitted often enough to strain the nerves of everyone present, by leaving the result in doubt until the last instant.

[1] American Archives V., vol. 2, col. 352.

[2] E. Wild's Journal; in Massachusetts Historical Society Proceedings, October, 1890, p. 119.

The whip was in some cases serviceable, although it had little effect upon the hardened offender, tied to a tree or post, who ground his teeth into a piece of lead and received the stinging blows in silence. When the prescribed number of stripes was administered in instalments, the flesh of the victim had time to become inflamed or to heal partially before the full penalty had been inflicted.[1]

Corporal punishment was carried out by the drummers and fifers under the eyes of the drum-major, who was required to be present.[2] Seventy-eight lashes were considered proper for a deserter and thirty-nine for a thief—a survival of the Mosaic number—but there was no invariable rule.[3] For writing "an infamous letter" against Colonel Brewer a soldier was sentenced to stand in the pillory for an hour where his comrades might witness his humiliation and suffering; in less than an hour he fainted.[4] Mr. Wild, our faithful chronicler, describes another scene—a soldier marching from the guard-house to the

[1] James Thacher's Military Journal, p. 223.

[2] *Ibid.*, p. 222 ; also Heath's General Orders, June 11, 1777.

[3] St. Paul said : Of the Jews five times received I forty stripes save one—II. Corinthians xi. 24.

[4] Paul Lunt's Diary, p. 13.

[174]

gallows with a halter about his neck, and from there running the gauntlet naked through the brigade.[1] Usually the brigade was drawn up in two lines to form a narrow lane (sometimes half a mile in length), through which the culprit had to pass to receive the lashing from switches held by the men. If he was unpopular he fared ill; if he was liked by his comrades and was fleet of foot he suffered but little. To make the gauntlet a serious penalty a soldier was ordered to point his bayonet at the guilty man's breast and back slowly down between the lines so that progress could not be too rapid for adequate punishment.[2] This ingenious device served to lay the victim on his bed for days.[3] At Ticonderoga a band of mutinous sailors ran a species of maritime gauntlet; they were sentenced to receive seventy-eight lashes each, " the criminals to be whip'd from vessell to vessell receiving Part of their Punishment on Board of each." [4] A more cruel punishment than most of those just mentioned was

[1] E. Wild's Journal ; in Massachusetts Historical Society Proceedings, October, 1890, p. 122.

[2] Rev. William Rogers's Journal, p. 123 ; James Thacher's Military Journal, p. 223.

[3] E. Hitchcock's Diary ; in Rhode Island Historical Society Publications, January, 1900, p. 211.

[4] Orderly Book of the Northern Army at Ticonderoga, p. 59.

that of riding the wooden horse, which so injured the man that some officers refused to make use of it.[1]

But there were penalties that afforded real amusement, as in the case of Bowen, sentenced to wear " a clogg chained at his legg " three days,[2] or in that of Griffith, guilty of selling Major Carnes's cordage, " to wear a clog four days with his coat turn'd rong side outwards." [3]

[1] Paul Lunt's Diary, p. 10 ; How's Diary, p. 32 ; A. M. Earle's Curious Punishments, p. 128.

[2] Essex Institute Collections, vol. 14, p. 67.

[3] *Ibid.*, p. 195.

VIII
Hospitals and Prison-Ships

THE Scylla and Charybdis of the soldier were the hospitals of his own army and the prison-ships of the enemy. Perhaps the knowledge of this made the life in camp and on the road more endurable than it would otherwise have been. To see the dawn over a hilltop drove out the depression that comes with the night, and to stand in the full radiance of the warm sun at noonday baffled malaria and stayed the march of disease. But the sun and the stars never came to the sufferer upon his sick-bed, nor often to the half-crazed, half-naked creature in his marine prison-pen.

The health of the men in camp was not forgotten, although the means of checking contagion and alleviating pain were inadequate, and many of the household remedies of to-day were then still to be discovered. In continued bad weather a half gill of rum was issued to each of the men, and they were cautioned against drinking new cider and also the water of streams forded during the heat of the day.[1]   The air of the huts and tents was purified by burning the powder of a blank musket cartridge daily, or by lighting pitch or tar;[2] the hospitals were treated in the same manner.

In many of the hospitals where there were few beds or blankets and no medicine or nurses, the service was not much more than the presence of a doctor until death came.   Colonel Wayne, writing to General Gates in December, 1776, said: "Our hospital, or rather house of carnage, beggars all description, and shocks humanity to visit.   The cause is obvious; no medicine or regimen on the ground suitable for the sick; no beds or straw to lay on; no covering to keep them warm, other than their own thin wretched clothing."[3]   At this time the deaths came so rapidly that the living grew weary of digging graves in the frozen earth.   "A scene something diverting, though of a tragic nature," as Lieutenant Elmer puts it, occurred in consequence.   Two graves had been dug with much labor by men of the New Jersey line for their

[1] Colonel William Henshaw's Orderly Book, p. 75.

[2] Washington's Orderly Book, May 26, 1778; Orderly Book of the Northern Army at Ticonderoga, p. 126.

[3] American Archives V., vol. 3, col. 1031.

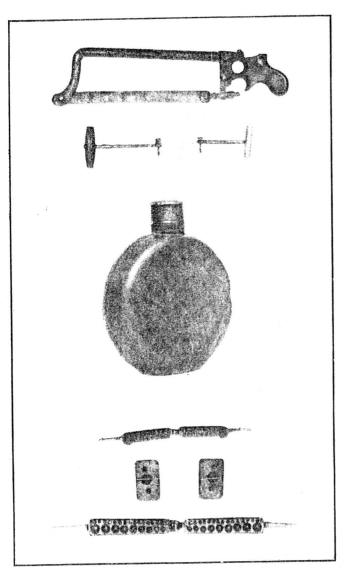

Surgeon's saw used by Dr. David Jones, who had been a student
under Dr. Joseph Warren. Teeth extractors (owned by the
Bostonian Society). Flask (owned by Mrs. R. W. Redman).
Revolutionary bullet moulds.

dead; but when they, having gone for the bodies, came back prepared to bury their comrades they found that some Pennsylvanians had come upon the open graves, and finding no one near, deposited their own dead there and covered them with earth. A hot dispute ensued and the New Jersey troops succeeded in digging up the other bodies, which were thrown under a heap of brush and stones.[1]

Good doctors and faithful ministers were rarely wanting in the camps; and they went about where men lay tossing from side to side on sacks of straw or grass, and did much to comfort the sufferers.

"My heart is grieved," wrote Rev. Ammi R. Robbins, "as I visit the poor soldiers—such distress and miserable accommodations. One very sick youth from Massachusetts asked me to save him if possible; said he was not fit to die: 'I cannot die; do, sir, pray for me. Will you not send for my mother? If she were here to nurse me I could get well. O my mother, how I wish I could see her; she was opposed to my enlisting: I am now very sorry. Do let her know I am sorry!'" Mr. Robbins was a devoted

[1] E. Elmer's Journal; in New Jersey Historical Society Proceedings, vol. 3 (1849), p. 93.

chaplain, who had to nerve himself constantly to bear the foul air that injured his health and the tales of sorrow that burdened his heart. He believed that the war was waged in a just cause, and when the men of whole congregations went out to battle, he felt that ministers should be ready to nurse their sick and bury their dead.[1]

At Saratoga an officer from each regiment was appointed weekly to visit every day the men from his own corps scattered through the hospitals.[2] But this care availed little when medicine and surgery were not always represented in camp by able physicians;[3] and antisepsis and anæsthetics were unknown. Cleanliness in conducting difficult operations was not insisted upon as it is to-day, and the wounds made by large round bullets moulded by hand needed the very best of treatment.[4] Putrefaction and pain ran riot in the emaciated bodies of the soldiers, and many who survived never regained their health.

The kind of medicine recommended by a doc-

[1] Robbins's Journal, p. 39.

[2] Orderly Book of the Northern Army at Ticonderoga, p. 123.

[3] American Archives V., vol. 3, col. 1584; Massachusetts Historical Society Proceedings, May, 1894, p. 88.

[4] G. L. Goodale's British and Colonial Army Surgeons, p. 10.

tor's wife may prove of interest. From a soldier's description of his sick friend's condition she
thought the trouble might be " gravels in the
kitteney," as the diarist wrote the name, and she
ordered a " quart of ginn and a tea dish of mus-
ter seed, and a hand full of horseradish roots—
steep them togather and take a glass of that every
morning." The gallant fellow submitted to this
new affliction, and happily was able to report
that " he found benefit by it." [1] The truth is that
much of the illness came from a longing to be at
home, from hunger, and from cold.   Referring
to the first of these causes of army sickness, General Schuyler once said : " Of all the specifics
ever invented there is none so efficacious as a discharge, for as soon as their faces turn homeward
nine out of ten are cured." [2]   For the other tenth,
just referred to, the remedy used at Valley Forge,
mutton and grog,[3] proved to be as useful as any-

[1] Elijah Fisher's Journal, p. 5.

[2] Schuyler to Congress, November 20, 1775 ; Lossing's
Schuyler (1872), vol. 1, p. 466.   Dr. Rush held to the view
that many New Englanders deserted on account of homesick-
ness.   When Gates met Burgoyne's army the excitement was a
strong power that overweighed fear and longing for home, so
that desertions for a few weeks almost ceased.   (Massachusetts
Magazine for 1791, p. 284.)

[3] Dr. A. Waldo's Diary ; in Historical Magazine, May,
1861, p. 133.

thing to aid in resisting the germs of disease that everywhere threatened the camp with pestilence. In the Quebec expedition, when exposure and hunger had prepared the way, a fourth or third of the men in some regiments died of small-pox.[1]

From the records of the general hospital at Sunbury, Penn., for 1777–80, it appears that about four-tenths of the patients (not counting the convalescents) were the wounded; about three-tenths suffered from diarrhœa or dysentery, and one-tenth from rheumatism.[2] To state this in another form, lack of proper food and shelter crippled the army as much as did the fire of the enemy. The number of cases treated, however, was not large enough to give very accurate statistics.

The sick suffered from crowding and from an insufficient supply of medical stores; those on the upper floors of hospitals had little or no ventilation, and at Bethlehem four or five invalids, one by one, occupied the unchanged straw until death came like an angel of mercy.[3] It is per-

[1] Charles Cushing, in American Archives V., vol. 1, cols. 128–132. See also letter of Council of Massachusetts to Ward, July 9, 1776, *ibid.*, col. 146.

[2] Pennsylvania Magazine, April, July, 1899, pp. 36, 210.

[3] Dr. William Smith; in Pennsylvania Magazine, July, 1896, pp. 149, 150.

haps not very strange that communities did not want army hospitals, and the arrival of open wagons in which lay groaning soldiers, wet with rain and snow, was the signal for vigorous protests from the populace. As soon as the patients were able to walk they were told that there was too little food to make a longer stay desired, and they were sent out penniless and weak to walk the country roads, begging from house to house.[1] This in itself was an objection to the presence of a hospital in a neighborhood.

In such a state of poverty the support of a minister seemed an expense that could be avoided, and few were found in the hospitals at New Windsor, West Point barracks, Morristown, Albany, Philadelphia, Fishkill, Yellow Springs, Williamsburg and Trenton, where many were often needed.[2]

Sickness and inadequate hospital facilities had a very direct effect upon the conduct of the war. Every haggard soldier who returned to the village of his birth was a silent force, decreasing enlistments and increasing the amount of bounty to be wrung from the taxpayers; this was particularly

[1] Director-General Cochran ; in Magazine of American History, September, 1884, p. 249.

[2] *Ibid.,* p. 257.

[183]

true at the South in the winter of 1776–77.[1]
The commissariat was the great arbiter of events
during the Revolution; insufficient food caused
disease and desertion, crippling the army until
Washington was forced to keep to a Fabian
policy that irritated those who were unfamiliar
with the obstacles in his path.

If the Continental soldier in the hospital of his
countrymen had reason for discontent, he might
well believe that he would fare even less happily
in the hands of the British, who rarely were able
to make adequate provision for their prisoners.
After the retreat from New York in 1776 the
churches of the town were crowded with starv-
ing Americans; some with dull eyes and parched,
speechless lips sat upright and sucked bits of
leather or wood—the last act of a reason almost
extinct, and others lay upon the bodies of their
comrades, gnawing bones and begging their
keepers to kill them.[2] While the helpless creatures were in this condition the sentries were said
to have annoyed them needlessly.[3] The descrip-

[1] Washington to Congress; in his Writings (Ford), vol. 5,
p. 241.

[2] E. Allen's Narrative, p. 34.

[3] American Archives V., vol. 4, col. 1234. See also E.
Fisher's Journal, p. 23.

[184]

tion of prison-life in Philadelphia during the British occupation is too ghastly to be credible in all its details. Dr. Albigence Waldo, of Washington's army, who has been quoted frequently in these pages, complained that the enemy did not knock their prisoners in the head, or burn them with torches, or flay them alive, or dismember them as savages do, but they starved them slowly in a large and prosperous city. One of these unhappy men, driven to the last extreme of hunger, is said to have gnawed his own fingers up to the first joint from the hand before he expired; others ate the mortar and stone which they chipped from their prison-walls, while some were found with bits of wood and clay in their mouths which in their death-agonies they had sucked to find nourishment.[1]

One must keep in mind the fact that nearly all contemporary authorities were influenced by the bitter spirit of the times to over-color their pictures of the suffering which came with war. There were frequent complaints of cruel treatment of prisoners from the commanders of both armies, British and American, and each side hoped to profit by the publicity given to harrowing de-

[1] Dr. A. Waldo's Diary; in *Historical Magazine*, May, 1861, p. 132.

tails. At about the time Americans were enduring privation in New York, in the autumn of
1776, an event occurred at the north which
proves that the British could show a magnanim-
ity that might become dangerous to the cause of
independence. Arnold's brave attempt to check
the advance of Sir Guy Carleton on Lake Champlain had ended in a furious naval fight and
Arnold's retreat. The American sailors taken by
Carleton were treated like friends by the commander and his men. News came to Gates that
they had been sent down the lake in boats to his
camp, and Colonel Trumbull was accordingly
instructed to meet them. Trumbull soon found
that the men were enthusiastic over their recep-
tion by Carleton and loudly praised the generosity
of the British. In alarm he hastened back to tell
Gates that the men would work mischief with
their tales of a bountiful enemy if allowed to
mingle with the soldiers of the army. Trumbull's
view was approved, and the surviving captives
were at once ordered southward to Skenesboro on
the way to their homes.[1]

The prison-ships were perhaps less oppressive
in summer than the city places of confinement;

[1] John Trumbull's Autobiography (New York, 1841), pp.
34–36.

[186]

but at best they were unclean, strictly guarded, and insufficiently supplied with food and medicine.[1] Many deaths occurred daily, and on board the Jersey (popularly known as Hell) the morning salutation of the officer was: " Rebels, turn out your dead!"[2] The horrors of those days have been pictured so often that it is unnecessary to re-sketch the sickening details. The living and the dead lay together in the stifling holds of the ships until the time came to bury the latter. These were put beneath the sand on the beach near by, and in the next severe storm they were washed back into the sea to float for days in the hot sun near the port-holes of the prison-ships. In warm weather one man was allowed on deck each night, and the prisoners crowded about the grating at the hatchway to get a breath of air and to be ready when their turn came to go out. The sentinels thrust their bayonets through the grating in sport, and sometimes, it is said, killed one of their prisoners.[3]

Lest these scenes in the lives of the captive

[1] American Archives V., vol. 3, col. 1138.

[2] Pennsylvania Packet, September 4, 1781 ; in F. Moore's Diary of the American Revolution, vol. 2.

[3] Martyrs of the Revolution in the British Prison-Ships in the Wallabout Bay, p. 19.

soldiers seem too incredible, it may be well to add the experiences of a man of letters who was famous in his day and is not altogether forgotten in our time—Philip Freneau, the poet of the Revolution. Freneau spent some time in the prison-ship Scorpion which lay in the North River in 1780. The conditions there were so terrible, according to the poet, that any plan of escape, however likely to fail, was tried; while every attempt increased the brutality of the Hessian jailers who were held responsible for their detention. When a number of men had rushed upon the sentries, disarmed them, boarded a vessel near by and escaped, the guards in their chagrin vented their anger upon the remaining prisoners by firing into the hatchways.

Freneau soon came down with a fever and was transferred to the hospital-ship Hunter. Some convalescents on board waited one day the coming of the doctor; when he had gone below they slipped into his boat as it lay alongside, and made a successful escape. The doctor was annoyed and after that, regardless of the sick and dying who had no part in the plan, he passed by the Hunter at a distance on his rounds. An appeal for "blisters," too loud to be ignored, one day caused him to rest on his oars; he looked up at the eager faces, suggested pleasantly that the sufferers plaster their backs with tar, and rowed on to the ill-famed Jersey.[1]

In a characteristic letter, written in 1780, from Passy, Dr. Franklin told Mr. Hartley, a peace-loving Englishman, that Congress had investigated these barbarities and had instructed him to prepare a school-book, to be illustrated by thirty-five good engravings, each one to picture a " horrid fact " that would impress the youthful posterity in America with the enormity of British malice and wickedness.[2]

While patriot soldiers were suffering in city prisons and on the water many captives were beginning years of confinement in Old Mill prison near Plymouth, England, and at Forton Gaol, outside Portsmouth. Usually they fared reasonably well, although forty days in a black hole, with half-rations and no resting-place but the damp stones, seems a severe penalty for attempting to escape, or for commenting unfavorably on the quality of the meat.[3] Isolated cases of barbarity were condemned in London newspapers,

[1] Philip Freneau's Capture of the Ship Aurora (1899), pp. 31–43.

[2] Franklin's Works (Bigelow), vol. 7, p. 5.

[3] Charles Herbert's Journal, edited by Livesey, p. 84.

and the frequent visits of Mr. Hartley, M.P., and Rev. Thomas Wren, of Portsmouth, to American prisoners, kept punishment within proper bounds. The people of London in December, 1777, subscribed £3,815 17s. 6d. to provide clothing and other necessities. A weekly allowance of two shillings from the American envoys was invaluable so long as it could be maintained, but in 1778 this was unavoidably reduced. The fare occasioned comparatively little protest, although Franklin, in his letters, complains that those who were not sold into service under the African or East India Companies were cheated by public prison contractors.[1] In 1780 he provided sixpence per week for each of the four hundred or more Americans, and as his countrymen were not permitted an equal allowance with the French and Spanish prisoners (being rebels), the money was very welcome. In the following year English generals sent home great numbers of captives; and Franklin's efforts to effect an exchange were thwarted by the caprice of British officials.

[1] Franklin's Works (Bigelow), vol. 9, pp. 108, 109. See also American Archives V., vol. 1, col. 754–756; Timothy Connor's Journal, edited by W. R. Cutter, in New England Historical and Genealogical Register, July, 1876, p. 345, July, 1878, pp. 280, 284 ; Gentleman's Magazine for 1778, p. 43.

Many remained captive in England for as long a period as four years, and when the general act for an exchange was passed, in the winter of 1782, there were more than a thousand Americans held for high treason in England and Ireland.[1]

The prisoners in some cases were allowed to make trinkets, which they sold to visitors, and they occasionally succeeded in sending letters to their friends. The news which was allowed to filter in was usually bad news, such as the final defeat of the Continentals, or the death of Washington.

In considering the British treatment of American prisoners in America some allowances must be made. The British army managed to cling to the sea-coast of the continent, but could not provide a suitable place in which to confine able-bodied captives who were ready at any time to effect an escape or to co-operate with an attempt made by the rebels to rescue them. The length of the war, also, bore hard upon the British soldiers, three thousand miles from home, and increased an irritation which perhaps received its first impulse from the regular's natural contempt for the volunteer in rebellion against the King.

[1] Franklin's Works (Bigelow), vol. 7, pp. 96, 306, 307, 451.

There were two ways of relief open to the prisoner in British hands, one at the sacrifice of his honor, another by the injury of his own cause : he could enlist under the crown, stifle his conscience, and take his chance of capture as a deserter; or he could—if fortunate—be exchanged for the redcoat in an American prison. Few of the better soldiers of native birth were willing thus to obtain freedom by service under the King; and the exchange of privates for privates operated so strongly to the advantage of the British forces that conference after conference could find no mutually satisfactory basis of agreement, and the prison-ships kept their burden. These prisoners, who had all the claims of humanity upon their side, were for the most part too enfeebled to be fit for further service, and some were levies called into the field for short periods. When exchanged, therefore, the sick would have to be discharged by Washington, and many of the able-bodied men, having reached the end of their terms of enlistment, would go home. The British captives, on the other hand, were better nourished, and less subject to disease; as they were in the regular army, they would remain in America, or be sent to do garrison duty in the place of troops that were being trained for service in the Colonies.[1] So it happened in this way that when Congress was hard pressed to keep in the field a force not too conspicuously inferior to the enemy, an exchange of prisoners was clearly a misfortune for every reason except that of humanity. As an exchange was a most practical means of " giving comfort to the enemy," the privates who endured year after year the hardships of prison and prison-ship, instead of going free, were serving their country as truly as if they had been in the field.

[1] Washington's Writings (Ford), vol. 8, p. 340 ; vol. 9, p. 445. Officers could be exchanged readily, and Washington at one time showed some anxiety to send back General Burgoyne lest ill-health should carry him off and deprive Congress of an opportunity to obtain in exchange for him 1,040 privates, or their equivalent in officers.—*Ibid.*, vol. 9, p. 219.

IX

The Army in Motion

SPRIGHTLY Sally Wister, arrayed in her prettiest clothes, watched Washington's army as it moved down the Skippack road from Germantown after the retiring red-coats; she enjoyed the " drumming, fifing and rattling of waggons," and the soldiers no doubt found pleasure in looking at her.[1]   In the bright sun and bracing air they made a gallant array; given the best of health and favorable roads they could march well for a number of miles, but much of the time bad roads and poor shoes retarded their progress, while broken sleep, wet clothing, or insufficient covering at night sapped the vitality of the best constitutions and made laggards of them all.   In rainy weather the baggage train, the artillery or the cattle, if they by any chance went before the men, cut the road to pieces and made it next to impossible to march in order.

[1] Sally Wister's Journal; in Jenkins's Historical Collections Relating to Gwynedd, p. 279.

A day's march in the Canada expedition was frequently as little as ten miles, while in Sullivan's campaign against the Indians the day's journey varied from less than ten to about twenty miles, although it at times rose to forty miles in the twenty-four hours.[1] Major Norris in his diary calls attention to the " most extrordinary march " of his men from Tioga to Easton in Pennsylvania, a distance of 156 miles, in eight days—nineteen miles a day—over a mountainous and rough wilderness, with artillery and baggage.[2] Better progress could be made by infantry when unencumbered; the Maryland companies of riflemen marched nearly 550 miles from Frederick Town (now Frederick City) to Cambridge in twenty-two days, or almost twenty-five miles a day.[3] General Greene's army in the Southern expedition covered 2,620 miles from April 16, 1780, to April 19, 1781 (Morristown to Camden), or about seven miles a day, including battles and camping.[4]

Men were often ordered at the Retreat or sunset

[1] Dr. Jabez Campfield's Diary, pp. 119, 121.

[2] James Norris's Journal; in Buffalo Historical Society Publications, vol. 1, p. 249.

[3] Daniel McCurtin's Journal; in T. Balch's Papers Relating to the Maryland Line (1857), pp. 11, 12.

[4] William Seymour's Journal; in Pennsylvania Magazine, December, 1883, p. 380 (vol. 7).

drum-beat to be ready to march at sunrise. At times the brigades paraded at sunrise, grounded arms, breakfasted, and if the weather was favorable, struck tents and marched by eight or ten o'clock; but occasionally the men fell into line at sunrise, were counted off, and marched from four to eight miles before breakfast. In the heat of the summer " the General " was beat frequently as early as two or three o'clock to warn the men that they were to march, and " the Troop" an hour later for them to fall into line.[1]

It was necessary to halt now and then for the artillery and stores to overtake the troops, or for the men to rest, wash their clothes, and clean their arms. When the long line was again in motion, sometimes in single file as happened in Sullivan's expedition, officers, musicians, rank and

[1] E. Wild's Journal, *passim*. Dictionaries differ in their definitions of *General* and *Troop*. Colonel Angell in his Diary (p. 106) says: " The Revelle beat as usual; the Genl at 5 oClock when the tents were struck; the Assembly at Six when [the] troops are paraded; the March at Seven when they all moved forward." Capt. Barnard Elliott's Diary (Charleston Year Book, 1889, p. 157) records the order "that when the assembly beats, to strike and pack up all the tents, load all the baggage, call in the quarter and the rear guards, and to stand to their arms." See also p. 236; and p. 245, where the long roll summoned the men to roll-call, and "the troop" meant that the new guard was to parade.

file, artillery, pack-horses, cattle and camp-follow-
ers, the spectacle was inspiring. As the 2,000
pack-horses in this expedition alone covered six
miles,[1] it is not difficult to understand that the
farmer on the lonely frontier might eat his breakfast as the first strains of music came down the
road, do his morning work and sit down to dinner
as the artillery came in sight, labor in the fields
and return to his supper as the rear-guard, in
search of stragglers, passed on.

The way through the Indian country was often
picturesque and strange, leading over high, barren mountains from which the wide plains, like
another world, could be seen below, then down
into wooded ravines, dark and damp with vapor.[2]
The men noticed the different trees, the pine,
the elm, the hemlock, the walnut, and turned
over the soil with their bayonets.[3] There was
much to see as Sullivan marched through the
country about the present Bradford, Penn., and
Elmira, N. Y., great stretches of "fine English
grass," spear-grass or clover,[4] and broad fields of

[1] Rev. William Rogers's Journal, p. 77.
[2] Jeremiah Fogg's Journal, p. 10.
[3] Dr. Jabez Campfield's Diary, p. 119.
[4] E. Elmer's Journal ; in New Jersey Historical Society Proceedings, vol. 2 (1846), p. 48.

maize, water-melons and pompions;[1] burning villages and smouldering corn-fields were on every
hand.

But such an expedition, necessary though it may
have been, gave no satisfaction to men who sought
worthy adversaries, and it demoralized those of
weaker character. "There is," said a surgeon
who understood the suffering that followed the
success of their army, "something so cruel in destroying the habitations of any people (however
mean they may be, being their all) that I might
say the prospect hurts my feelings."[2]

The soldiers passed the mangled bodies of two
dogs, hung high on poles to appease the evil spirit
that terrorized the red man and denied him victory.[3] The Spirit had not stopped the invaders,
who came upon the Indian camp-fires and villages
so rapidly that much was left behind in the haste
of flight. Near a hut they found a child of three,
weak and hungry but playing with a chicken,
while a milch cow, left by the not wholly heart-
less squaw, grazed quietly within sight, ready to

[1] Thomas Grant's Journal; in Historical Magazine, vol. 6,
pp. 235, 236.
[2] Dr. Jabez Campfield's Diary, p. 121.
[3] James Norris's Journal; in Buffalo Historical Society Publications, vol. 1, p. 246.

furnish nourishment.[1] A feeble old woman, left
by the Indians to the mercies of the white men,
received from General Clinton a keg of port and
some biscuit, although no officer of rank less than
a field officer had tasted such luxuries for some
days.[2] With this act of kindness must stand barbarities that would be incredible if noticed by a
single writer only. Lieutenant Barton, in his
Journal under the date August 30, 1779, says:
" At the request of Major Piatt, [I] sent out a
small party to look for some of the dead Indians—
returned without finding them. Toward morning
they found them and skinned two of them from
their hips down for boot-legs, one pair for the
Major, the other for myself." After reading of
this pleasant enterprise, which reached its successful consummation at a place near Cayuga Creek,[3]
it is not impossible to understand Thomas Anburey's observation that the Americans loved to
kill.[4]

There was, however, a brighter side to the war.
At " Seneca Castle," in a fertile country, the Ind-

[1] Jeremiah Fogg's Journal, p. 15.

[2] William Barton's Journal ; in New Jersey Historical Society
Proceedings, vol. 2 (1846), p. 39.

[3] *Ibid.,* p. 31.

[4] Anburey's Travels, vol. 1, p. 331.

ians were supposed to be gathered in force. As soon as the troops approached the woods and fields in the neighborhood, detachments were sent to the right and left and posted just out of sight, so that at a signal they could converge, hem in the savages, and take the works by storm. Having carefully arranged the details the general set out to inspect the lines before ordering an advance; as he rode he beheld each soldier with as many pompions or melons as his bayonet would hold, and each military shirt bulging with beans and corn. In his wrath he exclaimed: "You damned unmilitary set of rascals! What, are you going to storm a town with pompions?"

Some two weeks before the above event took place, the diarist whose account has been followed afforded amusement in a different way. In attempting to catch a doe which had ventured into camp he was knocked down and trod upon by the frightened creature in making her escape.[1] Deer, bears, and wild turkeys were not uncommon near Tunkhannock, Penn.,[2] but as the men

[1] Jeremiah Fogg's Journal, pp. 6, 14.

[2] W. Barton's Journal; in New Jersey Historical Society Proceedings, vol. 2 (1846), p. 26. Colonel I. Angell in his Diary (p. 101) relates that two deer went by his quarters in camp in New Jersey, December 12, 1779; the soldiers, not being allowed to fire, gave chase, but were unsuccessful.

were not allowed to fire in camp nor break ranks when marching, animals had little to fear. Pike, chub, gar and suckers were caught in the streams near where the army encamped.[1]

The southern campaigns brought other experiences. Pretty young women gathered at the roadside, says observant William Feltman, their faces almost entirely hidden by linen to protect them from the burning sun; and around them, as if in contrast, a retinue of blacks without a stitch of clothing to cover them.[2] A sight much more unpleasant, but possibly equally characteristic at the time, was that of a negro's head stuck on a sapling on one side of the road, and his right hand tied to a sapling on the opposite side. The negro had been hanged and cut in pieces for killing a white man.[3]

The same writer—an officer, but probably not more quick to receive impressions in a new country than some of the rank and file—comments on the lack of pines in North Carolina and Virginia, the infrequent meadows, and the flourishing plantations of the Germans and the Quakers. His

[1] James Norris's Journal; in Buffalo Historical Society Publications, vol. 1, p. 227.
[2] W. Feltman's Journal, p. 5.
[3] *Ibid.*, p. 30.

eye noticed the gray owl, the redbird, flocks of green paroquets and " samalligators "; and his ear detected sweet-singing frogs.[1]

If these wonders of nature were observed by the private soldier, he was less inclined to record them in his diary after the weary day's march and the meagre supper which followed; a tale of hardship and adventure was more suited to his laborious pen. James Melvin, a private in Arnold's unsuccessful expedition against Quebec in 1775, has described the ascent of the Kennebec into the heart of the Maine forests, and the journey down the Chaudière to the waters of the St. Lawrence. Death and desertion reduced the force of over 1,000 men to some 700, worn out by marches through " hideous woods," over mountains, and along the marshy banks of rivers, where the men sank into moss and mud, striving to haul the camp baggage through ravines and intervales. On October 28th they " waded knee-deep among alders &c., the greatest part of the way. . . One man fainted in the water with fatigue and cold, but was helped along. We had to wade into the water, and chop down trees, fetch the wood out of the water after dark to make a fire to dry ourselves; however, at last we

[1] W. Feltman's Journal, p. 37.

got a fire, and after eating a mouthful of pork, laid ourselves down to sleep round the fire, the water surrounding us close to our heads; if it had rained hard it would have overflown the place we were in."[1] Another member of the expedition has described the events of the next day: "We had to wade waist-high through swamps and rivers, breaking ice before us. Here we wandered round all day, and came at night to the same place which we left in the morning, where we found a small dry spot [and] made a fire; and we were obliged to stand up all night in order to dry ourselves and keep from freezing."

Three days later the same writer observed: [We] "travelled all day very briskly, and at night encamped in a miserable situation. Here we killed a dog, and we made a very great feast without bread or salt, we having been four days without any provisions; and we slept that night a little better satisfied. Our distress was so great that dollars were offered for bits of bread as big as the palm of one's hand."[2] The following day, staggering for want of food, they came upon the

[1] James Melvin's Journal, p. 5.
[2] Journal attributed to E. Tolman; in Massachusetts Historical Society Proceedings, April, 1886, p. 269.

cattle sent back by Colonel Arnold, who had gone on in advance of the party.

The camp-fire was the soldier's best friend on the march; by it he dried his clothes, and cooked his scanty meal; it protected him from the cold in northern countries, and even from prowling wild beasts. By its light he cleaned his gun, or wrote a few words in his diary for the family to read upon his return. While he slept it gave light to those who bridged the stream over which the army would pass at sunrise.[1] But if the camp-fire was a protection when the air at night was chilled by bleak winds and wet fog, there was no remedy for a tropical sun at noon. After the battle of Monmouth the army of Washington lay at English-Town for two days, and set out on July 1st for Spotwood; the weather was so warm that nearly a third of the men were unable to continue upon their feet until evening, and many had to be conveyed in wagons.[2] In Virginia in 1781 the troops were ordered to cut their coats shorter for their greater ease in marching under the hot sun.[3] The heat was somewhat

[1] Jeremiah Fogg's Journal, p. 11.

[2] Thomas Blake's Journal; in Kidder's First New Hampshire Regiment, p. 43.

[3] E. Wild's Journal, May 2, 1781; in Massachusetts Historical Society Proceedings, October, 1890, p. 137.

easier to bear than the cold; in the winter those
who had for shoes strips of rawhide (which were
passed under the soles and bound to the ankles)[1]
left marks of blood on the snow as they marched.[2]
Even those who had good shoes, sometimes kept.
them on for so long a time that the leather had to
be cut from their swollen feet.

The companionship of many men tramping
together was apt to keep fear from their minds;
but in passing through dark and lonely valleys at
night the dread of attack added to the gloom;
they sometimes marched in single file, each man
with his cartridge-box on his knapsack to keep it
dry in wading deep streams, and when on a dark
Indian trail each man with his hand on the frock
of the man before him to guide his steps.[3] The
rain beating ceaselessly upon the leaves overhead,
and dripping into the pools below; the wind
sighing and the wet branches creaking in the
wind; then a flash of lightning that revealed a
line of weary, muddy, plodding men—shut out
of sight in another instant by the black of night
and lost in the rumble and roar of thunder; that

[1] The Female Review (Dedham, 1797), p. 158.
[2] Heath's Memoirs (1798), p. 96.
[3] Nathan Davis's History; in Historical Magazine, April,
1868, p. 202.

was what a writer had seen when he wrote that " fighting happens seldom, but fatigue, hunger, cold & heat are constantly varying [the soldier's] distress." [1]   At such a time panic was ready to break forth at any moment.   On one occasion in Virginia, in May, 1781, the lightning struck near a moving column of troops and stampeded the horses.   The militia thought the enemy were upon them, threw down their arms in the muddy road where they were, and rushed headlong into the woods. [2]   The rear-guard, which was accustomed to follow the army to stop stragglers and deserters, sometimes performed a like duty over the cattle; and to march in the dark behind a thousand animals, along a narrow, muddy road, already cut to pieces by heavy artillery, was a test of patriotism.

A passage in the Journal of Elijah Fisher describes simply and well the hardships which the defensive policy of Washington, with its quick marches and counter-marches, brought upon the private soldier:

" About Dark it did begun to storm, the wind being at the N.E., and the Artillery went before

[1] Dr. Jabez Campfield's Diary, p. 119.

[2] E. Wild's Journal, May 29, 1781 ; in Massachusetts Historical Society Proceedings, October, 1890, p. 139.

The Army in Motion

and Cut up the roads; and the snow Come about
our shows [shoes] and then set in to rain, and
with all which made it very teges [tedious]. . .
At twelve at night we Come into a wood and
had order to bild ourselves shelters to brake
of [off] the storm and make ourselves as Com-
forteble as we could, but jest as we got a shelter
bilt, and got a good fire and Dried some of our
Cloths, and begun to have things a little Com-
furteble, though but poor at the best, thare Come
orders to march and leave all we had taken so
much pains for." [1]

There were brighter days and pleasant marches,
not to be left altogether from the soldier's calendar. A pretty story has been preserved by an
aged pensioner who was once in the Commander-in-chief's life-guard; it will serve to brighten
the picture of the army in motion. The men
were marching slowly along one day with Washington at their head. Where the road skirted a

[1] Elijah Fisher's Journal, p. 7. Thomas Blake's Journal
(Kidder's First New Hampshire Regiment in the war of the
Revolution, p. 37) pictures the greater suffering in time of retreat when he refers thus to Burgoyne's movements after the
second battle of Stillwater: "They burnt most of the buildings as they went, and cut away the bridges; and whenever
their wagons or tents or baggage broke down, they knocked the
horses on the head and burnt the baggage."

[207]

pond a number of boys were engaged in throwing or "jerking" stones to make them skim across the face of the water.

"Halt!" came the command. Then Washington said: "Now, boys, *I* will show you how to jerk a stone." He performed the feat successfully, smiled quietly, and ordered his men to march forward. That is the story, to be credited or not as one wills.[1]

When the soldiers endured every species of privation in camp and on the march, it is not strange that they treated the property of people near them somewhat cavalierly. As the Continentals came in sight, patriotic farmers drove their cattle into the hills and put their hens out of reach. To have their fellow-countrymen quartered upon them was distressing from the desolation that marked their sojourn.[2] Permission to take property was seldom granted to private soldiers, and Washington made every effort to appease the country-side. In an order against plundering, issued November 3, 1776, an exception was made in favor of straw, and, in time of great

[1] Alexander Milliner, in Hillard's Last Men of the Revolution, p. 42.

[2] W. Thompson's Deposition; in Publications of the Brookline Historical Publication Society, No. 12.

dampness, of grain in the sheaf, to keep the men from the ground at night.[1]   The custom of allowing scouting parties in time of great fatigue to take what they needed by plunder was greatly abused.

The Chevalier de la Luzerne relates that in the winter of 1779–80 the soldiers grew desperate under half-rations and took to marauding and pillage.   This was stopped by Washington, but as famine set in, he ordered foraging expeditions—house-to-house visitations—for clothing, blankets, shoes, and every kind of food that could be spared by non-combatants.   Under these trials of war the soldiery and the inhabitants seemed to the French writer very submissive.[2]   Needless cruelty the general abhorred,[3] and he strove constantly to suppress the baser element, which was as terrible a scourge as the enemy.[4]

Petty plunder was looked upon by the soldiers as " ragging " is to-day by college boys, a form of stealing that should be known by a more gentle name.   A soldier, for example, threw a stone at some geese in a pond, killed one, and stowed it

[1] Washington's Orderly Book, November 3, 1776.
[2] J. Durand's New Materials, p. 217.
[3] Washington's Orderly Book, July 7, 1776.
[4] Washington's Writings (Ford), vol. 4, p. 425.

away carefully in the roomy confines of his drum. When the irate farmer overtook the company the drum-head had been replaced and his search for the goose was unsuccessful. On another occasion the branches of a Quaker's orchard furnished some thirty or forty fowls, which were sent on ahead before daybreak, and later in the morning were cooked with onions, potatoes, and carrots.[1] When cattle grazed on the hill-side above the camp, and the kettle was empty, "a condition and not a theory" confronted the cook; in such a case a colonel was known not to disdain a quarter of beef left quietly at night beneath the flap of his tent. Or if a soldier (when meat was scarce) wished to visit a friend whom he had not seen for many years, and he was excused from roll-call by the captain, he might by chance find his "friend" in the act of cutting up a steer; it would be such a pleasure to return with meat for the company.[2]

Days of privation justified theft in the eyes of many of the rank and file. Upon one occasion, in 1779, the troops marched by the body of a soldier, hung for inexcusable treatment of the

[1] E. Fox's Revolutionary Adventures (1838), pp. 49, 51.

[2] John Shreve's Personal Narrative; in Magazine of American History, September, 1879, p. 575.

people. A comrade slapped the dead man on the thigh and said: "Well, Jack, you are the best off of any of us—it won't come to your turn to be hanged again this ten years."[1]

In the north sympathizers with the King suffered less at the hands of passing soldiers than in the south; and yet it was not uncommon for a plain-spoken Tory—a "ministerial tool"—to get a coat of tar and feathers, especially during the months when companies from the central colonies were on their way to join the army about Boston.[2] The British regulars in Boston as early as March, 1775, had inflicted like punishment on a country fellow who (as was said) had been making preparation for rebellion by buying a gun from a red-coat.[3]

Tories were not always subjected to tar and feathers; in May, 1776, at a drinking "frolic," as it was called, a Tory forgot his caution and drank to the King's success; he was immediately dragged off to the guard, who knocked

[1] E. Hitchcock's Diary ; in Rhode Island Historical Society Publications, January, 1900, p. 223.

[2] Aaron Wright's Revolutionary Journal ; in Historical Magazine, July, 1862, p. 209 ; also William Hendrick's Journal ; in Pennsylvania Archives, 2d series, vol. 15, p. 28.

[3] John Rowe's Diary ; in Massachusetts Historical Society Proceedings, March, 1895, p. 90.

the end out of a hogshead and forced him to "dance Yankee Dudle in it untill next day." [1]

In the south there was no neutral ground possible for the country people. When the King's troops were in possession of the land, the Tories drove the rebel sympathizers into the mountains, killing husbands on their doorsteps and shooting children before their helpless mothers. When Lincoln or Gates or Greene came down from the north the tide of blood swept back upon the Tories.

Many families in Georgia and elsewhere on this account lived in the mountains and subsisted by hunting. [2] Efforts were made, however, to protect the royalists, and General Greene in his orders prohibited the soldiery from insulting any of the inhabitants "with the odious epithets of ' Tory' or any other indecent language, it being ungenerous, unmanly and unsoldierlike." [3] In truth, the poor Tories found little comfort from either army; a New York fugitive declared that the British spoke of the enemy as rebels, but the Tories they called " damned traitors and scoun-

---

[1] D. McCurtin's Journal; in T. Balch's Papers (1857), p. 40.

[2] Luzerne, in J. Durand's New Materials, p. 252.

[3] Colonel Hutchinson's Orderly Book, p. 7.

drels." In many towns they were forced to drill with their neighbors, and when drafted, were expected to pay well for substitutes;[1] in Massachusetts the selectmen or overseers of the poor were empowered to bind out their children with those of the town paupers.[2]

The Tory while an exile in England suffered in spirit if he escaped physical pain; he heard his native land referred to in pompous terms as *our* plantations, and, as Franklin so delightfully drew the picture, he saw every Englishman "jostle himself into the throne with the King" that he might talk of *our subjects in the colonies.*[3] His friends in the rebel army were said to possess "every bad quality the depraved heart can be cursed with." Before he could analyze his thoughts he found himself rejoicing that news of a rebel victory diminished the conceit of the insufferable "Islanders" about him; and it may be said that the Tory in a foreign land never entirely forgot that his friends and his kinsmen were fighting for the soil that he loved. Curwen has shown us these feelings in the story of his own exile,[4] and Governor

[1] American Archives V., vol. 1, col. 356.
[2] *Ibid.,* vol. 1, col. 286.
[3] Franklin's Works (Bigelow), vol. 4, p. 3.
[4] American Archives V., vol. 3, col. 1269.

Hutchinson wished to return to lie at last in the soil of his native land.[1]

The practice of plundering Tories was not so much to be regretted as that of robbing the friends of Congress under the specious pretence that they were secretly loyal to the crown. This habit annoyed Washington frequently, and he complained in January, 1777, to the governor of New Jersey, that the militia officers had been known to lead their men in these infamous expeditions.[2] But robbery was a misfortune less serious than the treatment received by real Tories. The Council of Bennington in January, 1778, gave out the following order:

" Let the overseer of the tories detach ten of them, with proper officers to take the charge, and march them in two distinct files from this place through the Green Mountains, for breaking a path through the snow. Let each man be provided with three days' provisions; let them march and tread the snow in said road of suitable width for a sleigh and span of horses; order them to return, marching in the same manner, with all convenient speed. Let them march at 6 o'clock tomorrow morning." [3]

[1] T. Hutchinson's Diary and Letters (London, 1886), vol. 2, pp. 257, 335.

[2] Washington's Writings (Ford), vol. 5, p. 201 ; also his Revolutionary Orders (Whiting), p. 70.

[3] Note in Hadden's Journal, p. 128.

After the battle of Bennington the Tories were
the sport of the soldiery; they were tied together
in pairs, and attached by the traces to horses
which were in some cases driven by negroes.[1]
The same spirit is evident in the remark of a
soldier, made after the battle: "One Tory, with
his left eye shot out, was led by me, mounted on
a horse who had also lost his left eye. It seems to
me cruel now—it did not then."[2] If the thought
and action of the time appear unworthy of men
fighting for liberty, it is well to stand for a moment as they did, with the contemptuous red-coat
and his prison-ship toward the rising sun, and
the treacherous redskin with his scalping-knife
toward the western sun: that was no time for
over-refinement.

The British army, while marching through an
enemy's country, found the Indian allies un-
manageable; they demanded permission to pillage and torture as their reward for service. Perhaps with this in mind General Fraser told his
prisoners that if they attempted to escape they
would receive no quarter, but would be at the
mercy of Indians, to be hunted down and scalped.
Probably Fraser hardly expected to be forced to

---

[1] Memoir of General John Stark, by C. Stark, p. 63.

[2] J. D. Butler's Bennington address, p. 29.

allow so barbarous a punishment, but Burgoyne himself found the greatest difficulty in holding the savage allies to humane methods of warfare and regard for prisoners. Thacher has described the art of scalping. " With a knife," he writes, " they make a circular cut from the forehead, quite round, just above the ears ; then taking hold of the skin with their teeth, they tear off the whole hairy scalp in an instant, with wonderful dexterity." [1] This operation, very serious and painful, was not necessarily fatal, and a number of soldiers survived the scalping-knife as they did battles and lived into the next century. After the fight at Freeman's Farm the Indians are said to have spent the next morning in scalping the dead and wounded ; a German officer makes the statement, and when taken with other evidence it does not seem improbable. Scalps were worth about eight dollars each, the price varying somewhat, according to agreement.[2] General Carleton has been accused of paying for scalps, and American prisoners of more or less veracity, as well as Indians, testified to this as a fact.[3] While it can scarcely be credited as con-

[1] James Thacher's Military Journal, p. 137.

[2] J. Priest's Stories of the Revolution, p. 19.

[3] J. Melvin's Journal, p. 23 ; also American Archives V., vol. 2, col. 268.

sistent with Carleton's known character or as probable treatment of white people by their own race, one should not forget that the colonists had for a century and more set a dangerous example.

A bounty on scalps of hostile Indians was the prize toward which a frontier "centinel" looked to augment his income. As an instance among many the vote of the New Hampshire House of Representatives. May 7, 1746, may be given. The tariff was fixed at seventy pounds for the scalp of each male Indian over twelve who was at war with the province, and of thirty-seven pounds and ten shillings for scalps of women and of *children under twelve years of age.*[1] Had the Indians joined the American army they would have scalped the British regulars who took their chances of death in any form; but they threw in their lot with the royal cause, and so fell upon old men, helpless women and children more often than they did upon the Continentals. These were the unfortunate conditions of the struggle.

There is little to relieve these pictures of barbarity, and yet the following sprightly narrative

[1] New Hampshire Provincial Papers, vol. 5, p. 410.

by Ethan Allen is not without its humorous aspect. He says:

" The officer I capitulated with, then directed me and my party to advance towards him, which was done; I handed him my sword, and in half a minute after, a savage, part of whose head was shaved, being almost naked and painted, with feathers intermixed with the hair of the other side of his head, came running to me with an incredible swiftness; . . . malice, death, murder, and the wrath of devils and damned spirits are the emblems of his countenance; and in less than twelve feet of me presented his firelock; at the instant of his present, I twitched the officer, to whom I gave my sword, between me and the savage; but he flew round with great fury, trying to single me out to shoot me without killing the officer; but by this time I was nearly as nimble as he, keeping the officer in such a position that his danger was my defence; but in less than half a minute I was attacked by just such another imp of hell: Then I made the officer fly around with incredible velocity for a few seconds of time, when I perceived a Canadian who had lost one eye, as appeared afterwards, taking my part against the savages, and in an instant an Irishman came to my assistance with a fixed bayonet, and drove away the fiends, swearing by Jesus he would kill them." [1]

[1] Ethan Allen's Narrative (Philadelphia, 1779), p. 11.

X

The Private Himself

THE Revolutionary rank and file, when their uniforms were fresh, were a picture for the eye, with their cocked hats decked with sprigs of green, their hair white with flour, their fringed hunting shirts, and their leather or brown duck breeches. Many were boys; some at the opening of the war were under sixteen, with the virtues and vices of youth. They were eager for adventure, and every strange sight and custom made its impress upon them. In the Quebec expedition the way-side crosses and the chapel interiors, rich in color, interested the soldiers; in the march against the Six Nations, Indian superstitions and habits of life were described in almost every diary, and in the southern colonies the peculiarity of slavery attracted the attention of the men from the north. Through travel and contact with the world there was an opportunity for the earnest soldier of good principles to widen his horizon and broaden his sympathies: the Yankee, the Dutchman, and the Southerner came to know more of one another.

Some of those who could write kept diaries. These journals have many references to the weird and the unusual, and they show a rough humor. In this respect they reflect the taste of the time. Privates, even those who rose to the commissioned ranks, spelled many words by sound. When this spelling indicates peculiarities in pronunciation it gives some impression of the language of the camp-fire. David How, of Methuen, was a private of the Massachusetts line, with all the sharpness and oddities that characterize a New England farmer. In his diary there is a consistency of error which amounts to a dialect. He always wrote *whept* for whipped, and the same tendency is evident in the use of *splet* meaning split, *steant* for stint, and *a pecking up* for picking up. A New Englander, therefore, seems to have pronounced short *i* as though it had the sound of *e* in get; he reversed the sounds in words which properly have short *e*, saying *ridgment* for regiment, *git* for get, *wint* instead of went, *lit* for let, etc. Private John White, also a New Englander, used *a* for *e* and *i* so persistently that the nasal twang is very evident, as in his use of *sarten* for certain, *prants* for prints, *lave* for leave, *sands* for sends, and *wall* for well.[1]

Privates How and Fisher treated *r* much as it is treated to-day in New England. They wrote *Salletoga* for Saratoga, *Dodgster* for Dorchester, *soyloin* for sirloin, *yestoday* for yesterday, and *afte* instead of after ; but where no *r* occurs or where it is not emphasized they made it prominent, by writing *for teag* in place of fatigue, *cateridges* for cartridges (always), *arams* for arms, *warter* for water, and *carstle* for castle. Other pronunciations, as *valible* for valuable, *bargon* for bargain, *jine* for join, and *jest* for just are not uncommon to-day. "Privateer" was a stumbling-block that had to be overcome in those exciting days, and How bravely wrote "privitesters," and "priviteteres" to convey his meaning. Phrases now unused appear in diaries, as "lit of," meaning met, "for to go to Boston," and "sase money" (an allowance for vegetables). The impression which proper names made upon the mind of a private soldier may be inferred from his use of Hushing (Hessians), Dullerway (Delaware), Vinkearne (Lincoln) and Markis Delefiat or Delefiatee. It should not be forgotten, however, that on the whole the English language as

[1] Parmenter's Pelham, Massachusetts, p. 129.

[221]

spoken by the more educated colonists was purer than the speech of Englishmen whose lives were confined to such counties as Devon and Yorkshire.[1]

The soldiers had their own designations for their enemies and friends; the British were commonly called " lobsters," [2] and new recruits were, it is said, spoken of as " the long-faced people." [3]

Keeping a diary in all kinds of weather, with no table to write upon, poor quills and thick ink, and hands numb with cold, or stiff from guard duty, was an achievement which must command respect. As the scratchy pen was driven slowly across the fibrous paper in the flickering glare of the camp-fire, the writer, with brows puckered to

[1] See Franklin's Works (Bigelow), vol. 4, p. 246.

[2] The term " lobsters " is said to have been applied in 1643 to cuirassiers on account of their bright armor (Notes and Queries, September 24, 1859, p. 252); later it was perhaps suggested by the color of the British coats (*ibid.*, April 8, 1876, p. 286; October 6, 1900, p. 266; December 29, 1900, p. 516).

[3] Military Journals of Two Private Soldiers, pp. 57, 65, 80, etc. This interpretation is given by the editor of the diary. Mr. Albert Matthews has called my attention to the following phrase in Moore's Diary, vol. 1, p. 350 : " We intend to push on after the long-faces in a few days." This seems to refer to the American troops, and possibly the words had a still more specific meaning.

concentrate his thoughts and keep from his mind
a babel of voices, put down much that was in-
structive and amusing. To one the Sunday text
was worthy of note, to another the current price
of shoes or the details of an execution for crime.
Mr. How was careful to record deaths, and after
each name a heavy black line completed the
entry as a proper mark of mourning. Sam
Haws, of Wrentham, was particular about the
appearance of his pages, and when he made a
blot in his Journal he added: "o you nasty
Sloven how your Book Looks."[1]

Elijah Fisher, referred to above, studied diligently when opportunity offered. His diary, in
February, 1780, states: "I stayes [with Mr.
Wallis] and follows my Riting and sifering the
same as I had Dun the Evnings before, for Every
Evning from six of the Clock till Nine I used to
follow my study." Under date of October 17th
this quaint note appears in his book : "I agreed
with Sarjt Sm. Whippels to stay one month with
him after my time was out and so do his Duty
and he was to larn me to Rite and sifer and
what other larning would be eassy." It is pleasant to know that this training proved of value
the next year, when the absence of the captain,

[1] Military Journals of Two Private Soldiers, p. 82.

one lieutenant, and both sergeants for a time threw much of the care of the company upon his shoulders.[1]

The retreat from Bunker Hill was mortifying to the defeated participants, officers as well as men, who found fault with the insufficient powder and reënforcements. The Americans were on a peninsula the approach to which could be commanded by a British man-of-war. They did not realize that longer occupation might have induced the British to cut off their line of escape and starve them into surrender. A quick defeat for which the enemy paid heavily both in lives and in prestige did more for America than possession of the defences on the hill for another night could possibly have done. Until a soldier acquired sufficient education to fit him for an officer's commission he was not thrown with men who heard the current news at head-quarters; his horizon, therefore, was limited, and a battle, far reaching in its influence upon events, meant no more to him than a chance encounter.

A private at the battle of Long Island, ignorant of the critical state of the patriot cause on

<hr />

[1] E. Fisher's Journal, p. 17.

that memorable occasion, states the facts very quietly:

27. Our army on long Island Have ben Engaged in battle With the Enimy and Kill^d And taken a good many on Both sides.

29. This night our army on long Island All left it & Brought all their Bagage to N. York.[1]

The same soldier thus described the battle of Trenton:

26. This morning at 4 a Clock We set off with our Field pieces Marchd 8 miles to Trenton Whare we ware Atacked by a Number of Hushing [Hessians] & we Toock 1000 of them besides killed Some Then we march^d back And got to the River at Night And got over all the Hushing.

28. This Day we have ben washing Our things.[2]

The writer declined to heed the general's entreaty to remain in service for six weeks longer, drew his wages and " sase money," and marched for home, missing by two days the famous engagement at Princeton. The soldier's inability to comprehend the state of affairs at critical periods may account often for a seeming lack of patriotism, as in the case just cited, but on the other hand his ignorance kept his heart light. Colonel

---

[1] David How's Diary, p. 26.   [2] *Ibid.*, p. 41.

Cadwalader, less than a fortnight before the battle of Trenton, closed a letter to Robert Morris by saying that he had been led into a complaining tone " by the d——d gloomy countenances seen wherever I go except among the soldiers." [1]

When given a chance the privates did their share of thinking; in the execution of large plans this was a disadvantage, since the machine-like corps could better be reckoned with than the body of individuals. In 1776 a skirmish took place between a party of straggling soldiers and some Hessians who held a rocky eminence between the termination of Mount Washington and King's Bridge. Two Pennsylvania privates advanced up the hill and opened fire; they were soon joined by a few recruits, who soon silenced the Hessian guns. Seeing this, a detachment of about fifty of the enemy set off to aid their outposts. By this time the little group of volunteers numbered twenty or more; without officers to conuslt, they talked over the matter among themselves, and decided to form into three divisions, one to attack the rocky defences of the enemy and two to circle the position in order to fall upon it in the rear or to meet the advancing reënforcements. The manœuvre was entirely successful, for the outpost

[1] American Archives V., vol. 3, col. 1231.

retreated to avoid falling into the trap, and the Americans took and held the rocky stronghold until darkness came on.[1]

In any large number of men some there are who will study and think for themselves, ready or preparing to influence and lead; but too many are indolent and heedless. When Mrs. Esther Reed in 1780 offered to Washington the 300,634 paper dollars which the ladies of Philadelphia had raised for the army, she proposed to turn this sum into specie and present to each soldier two " hard " dollars. The Commander replied that he preferred a shirt for each man, as money would induce drinking and discord.[2] The payment of wages often led to disorder, as intimated by a private at Cambridge in his remark: " Peace with our enemy, but disturbance enough with rum, for our men got money yesterday." [3]

Rum was an article of daily consumption, and its evil effects must have balanced whatever of good it did. It was drunk " to the health and success of the ladies," [4] to celebrate victories, to

[1] American Archives V., vol. 3, col. 602.

[2] Life of Joseph Reed, vol. 2 (1847), pp. 262–266.

[3] Aaron Wright's Revolutionary Journal ; in Historical Magazine, July, 1862, p. 210.

[4] Military Journals of Two Private Soldiers, p. 57.

encourage enlisting, by fatigue parties to counter-
act the strain of hard work in bad weather, and
even more liberally when there was no object in
view; when taken early in the morning, unmixed
with water, it impaired the health of the men;[1]
and in long marches the hard drinker was most
apt to suffer.[2]   At the siege of Boston Sam Haws,
a private, experienced the not unusual effects of
merry-making.   " We turned out," he says, " and
went to the Larm post and it was very cold, and
we came home and there was a high go of Drinking Brandy, and several of the company were
taken not well pretty soon after."[3]   David How
tells the story of two men at Cambridge who fell
to bantering one another as to who could drink
the most.   This led to excessive drinking, from
which one of the men died in an hour or two.[4]
Upon another occasion John Coleman " drinkt 3
pints of cyder at one draught,"[5] a feat that excited
comment.   James McDaniel was so eager for rum
that he forged an order to obtain it.[6]   To check

[1] Colonel Hutchinson's Orderly Book, p. 15.

[2] Dr. E. Elmer's Journal ; in New Jersey Historical Society
Proceedings, vol. 2 (1846), p. 48.

[3] Military Journals of Two Private Soldiers, p. 78.

[4] D. How's Diary, p. 5.

[5] Military Journals, p. 70.

[6] Colonel William Henshaw's Orderly Book, p. 59.

excessive drinking, spirits were allowed to be sold in one place only within the limits of each brigade, and sutlers were sometimes enjoined from selling after the retreat had been sounded at sunset.[1]

Hard cider was much used, as it still is in country towns, in place of distilled liquors. The story is told of a private, then not over sixteen years of age, who was taunted in camp with being homesick until he lost his patience and attempted to thrash his persecutor. At first unsuccessful, he called for quarter, but, receiving none, he fought desperately and worsted his antagonist. The affair became the talk of the company and reached the ears of the captain. The two men—boys they really were—soon came up before their comrades to receive whatever public punishment the captain thought meet. Amid silence he looked sternly at the culprits, angular and tall, poorly clad by their province, and as poorly fed, youthful and perhaps a little frightened; he allowed his eyes to rest on their bronzed faces, for he knew them well; then in the hush he said, " You are ordered for punishment to drink together a mug of cider." After the first instant's astonishment the laughter that followed was proof that the captain knew the failings of his men.

[1] Jonathan Burton's Orderly Book, p. 13.

Sensuality is not often mentioned in the diaries or letters of the soldiers, although references are not wanting. Stealing, however, was not uncommon. Lieutenant Burton lost his "cotten" shirt by a " bold Theefe ";[1] and a soldier for stealing a cheese was whipped thirty lashes.[2] Samuel Haws has related how in the camp near Boston, in October, 1775, a " Rifle man [was] whipt 39 stripes for Stealing and afterwards he was Drummed out of the camps; if the infernal regions had ben opened and cain and Judas and Sam Haws had been present their could not have ben a biger uproar."[3]

Swearing was a habit which Washington tried in vain to check; the coarse language of many of the men shocked him as it did others. A clergyman, referring to the New York troops who were with Arnold in 1776, remarked that " it would be a dreadful hell to live with such creatures forever."[4] But to suppose that there was no strong religious leaven in the army would be a mistake. Corporal Farnsworth, of Groton, found a young soldier with whom he could converse freely on

[1] Jonathan Burton's Orderly Book, p. 36.
[2] David How's Diary, p. 12.
[3] Military Journals of Two Private Soldiers, p. 76.
[4] Rev. A. R. Robbins's Journal, p. 10.

spiritual things, and said, with a grateful heart: " I find God has a Remnant in this Depraved and Degenerated and gloomy time." [1]

While every army has its men of low principles, they weigh little in the winning or losing of campaigns if the great majority are efficient and brave.

The Americans as a pioneer people were accustomed to danger, and they were familiar with fire-arms.[2] Men might be relegated to the "awkward squad" to learn manners,[3] but the polish would cover a stout heart. Sir William Johnson wrote that the British ministry must not look upon the Americans as cowards who would not fight;[4] while Anburey commented on their "courage and obstinacy," which had already astonished the officers under Burgoyne.[5] A Continental soldier who had been at Bunker Hill remarked that he would to God that his people had as good courage in the spiritual warfare as they had in the

[1] Amos Farnsworth's Diary; in Massachusetts Historical Society Proceedings, January, 1898, p. 85.

[2] J. Durand's New Materials, p. 25; American Archives V., vol. 3, col. 1395.

[3] A. Lewis's Orderly Book, p. 6; also Military Journals of Two Private Soldiers, p. 54.

[4] Johnson's Orderly Book, p. 49, note.

[5] T. Anburey's Travels, vol. 1, p. 418.

temporal.[1]   Not to multiply statements, the testimony of a Tory of New York may be given as final evidence of reasonable courage shown by the American troops; commenting on the fighting in New Jersey in June, 1780, he remarked of the rebels: " They were mostly militia, and stood and fought better than ever before."[2]

No doubt the militia accomplished all that could be fairly expected of men who did not make war a profession.   They were subject to panic, but fought well when they knew the land and the purpose of the commander, and were also sure that no trap awaited them.   A saying in the army that Gates loved the militia because they would never bring him under fire is a commentary on the private as well as the general.[3]   But men who were familiar with militia knew what to expect. Dr. John Witherspoon, of New Jersey, speaking in Congress in 1776, reminded the members that at the battle of Preston militia ran like sheep; at Falkirk, in 1746, the speaker himself saw troops

[1] A. Farnsworth's Diary ; in Massachusetts Historical Society Proceedings, January, 1898, p. 87.

[2] E. G. Schaukirk's Diary ; in Pennsylvania Magazine of History and Biography, vol. 10, p. 431.

[3] E. Hitchcock's Diary ; in Rhode Island Historical Society Publications, January, 1900, p. 224.

"behave fifty times worse" than the Americans had behaved at Long Island.

Washington said of his own troops in 1776: "Place them behind a parapet, a breast-work, stone wall, or any thing that will afford them shelter, and from their knowledge of a firelock, they will give a good account of their enemy; but I am as well convinced, as if I had seen it, that they will not march boldly up to a work nor stand exposed in a plain." [1] A few months later he wrote: "Being fully persuaded that it would be presumption to draw out our young troops into open ground against their superiors both in number and discipline, I have never spared the spade and pickaxe. I confess I have not found that readiness to defend even strong posts at all hazards, which is necessary to derive the greatest benefits from them." [2] Washington wrote these words after the battle of Long Island.

Five days later Lord Percy wrote: "The moment the Rebels fired, our men rushed on them with their Bayonets & never gave them time to load again. . . . I think I may venture to assert, that they will never again stand be-

[1] Washington's Writings (Ford), vol. 3, p. 398.
[2] *Ibid.*, vol. 4, p. 392.

fore us in the Field." [1] Whether this was due to cowardice or inexperience he did not assert, but Curwen, the loyalist, held to the view that the inability of untrained troops to face regulars in the open was no proof of lack of bravery.[2]

It has been said that Washington's strength as a commander lay in his readiness to learn a lesson from experience. He discovered very soon the value of earthworks, and persisted in their use without regard to expressions of disapproval from European officers. In Braddock's campaign his advice to seek protection behind trees had met with disfavor, and now Lee spoke slightingly of hastily made defences, and others considered them destructive of manliness and courage. John Adams represented a certain public impatience when he wrote : " The practice we have hitherto been in, of ditching round about our enemies, will not always do. We must learn to use other weapons than the pick and the spade." [3]

The motives which controlled enlistment are

[1] Percy's Letters ; in Boston Public Library Bulletin, January, 1892, pp. 325, 326.

[2] American Archives V., vol. 3, col. 1306. Franklin in 1769 wrote a vigorous defence of the provincial militia in answer to a taunting article in No. 310 of the London Chronicle. See his Works, edited by Bigelow, vol. 4, p. 247.

[3] American Archives V., vol. 1, col. 103.

not easily defined; patriotism, adventure, money, glory, all have their weight in determining human action. A Frenchman who spent a year in America reported that all the recruits were mercenaries, led by a few patriotic officers.[1] So general a charge needs no serious answer, but it may be stated as self-evident that the poorer the soldier of any rank, the more dependent he will be upon the compensation which he receives for his services. The rank and file were no doubt more in need of money than their officers; when it did not come, even in the form of paper, they mutinied; their officers, fortunately, could resign. The charge could not have been true in 1775; later, as it became evident that farmers with children to be supported were unable to remain in the army, their places were taken by young men who made war a profession and expected its rewards.

The heads of families soon found that service in the army meant starvation for those at home. Through the demands of producers, following the example set by avaricious retailers, the price of necessities rose beyond the reach of the soldiers' wives. Said a student of the times: "At this rate what will become of thousands of people who depended on their absent friends in the army

[1] J. Durand's New Materials, p. 25.

[235]

for a subsistence?" Those who, having no home ties, could go into the army for a small bounty and moderate wages, were carried along by the tide; what the married men required, the young men, seeing their opportunity, were led to demand.[1]

Claude Blanchard visited the army under Washington at Peekskill in 1781; to his eye the soldiers marched well but handled their arms badly. "There were," he relates, "some fine-looking men; also many who were small and thin, and even some children twelve or thirteen years old. They have no uniforms, and in general are badly clad."[2] It is not difficult to understand the physical condition of men who had clung to army life through its few bright days, and its many days of privation, when one recalls the winter at Valley Forge. It was there that James Thacher, while walking with Washington among the soldiers' huts, heard voices echoing through the open crevices between the logs, "no pay, no clothes, no provisions, no rum"; and the few who flitted from hut to hut were covered only with dirty and ragged blankets.[3]

[1] American Archives V., vol. 3, col. 1176 (year 1776).
[2] Blanchard's Journal, p. 115.
[3] J. Thacher's Military Journal, p. 154.

Head-Quarters Valley-Forge. January 1. 1778.

Parole Ulster — C. Signs {Salem.
{Amboy. —

As this day begins the new year The General orders a gill of spirits
to be served to each non commission'd Officer & soldier; And to
avoid the irregular and partial distribution of this Article
which has been a good deal complaind of) he expressly
orders that no spirits shall issue to any part of the troops in
future but in Consequence of general or special orders from
Head Quarters — A deviation from this rule will be at the
risque and peril of the Issuing Commissary. —

Return of the Commanding Officer of each Regiment is to give in
a Return at orderly time tomorrow of the number of Taylors
in the Regiment he commands; and no new Cloathing to be
made for the use of any Regiment but by a pattern which
will be furnished them. —

A considerable number of Frocks and some Axes are
ready to be issued at the Quarter Master Generals Stores —

Col. Cook is appointed President of the Court Martial
which sits daily at the Bake-House; to relieve Col. Brearm
molle. —

Celebration of New Year's Day.
Page from Washington's order book, Jan. 1, 1778.

The men were supposed to make as good an appearance on guard and at parade as was possible. They were ordered to have their beards close shaved, their clothes and shoes cleaned,[1] and their faces and hands washed.[2] When an event of importance occurred the men powdered their hair. South Carolina troops, in 1776, were instructed to have their hair "properly trimmed up and tyed for cap wearing, but without side locks." Pay for the barbers was obtained by stoppages from the wages of the men.[3] In our day powder and long hair seem more suited to a ball-room than a battle-decimated army. The convenience and cleanliness of short hair did not, apparently, receive the serious attention of commanding officers.

Sullivan's army, 3,000 strong, returned from the Indian country in tatters, "with the remaining parts of their garments hanging in streamers behind them," yet they had sprigs of evergreen in their caps, and their heads were as white as a wagon-load of flour could make them. The incongruity of the spectacle convulsed the

[1] A. Lewis's Orderly Book, pp. 8, 27.
[2] Jonathan Burton's Orderly Book, p. 17.
[3] Captain Barnard Elliott's Diary ; in Charleston Year Book, 1889, p. 188.

officers and moved the chaplain "to forget his gravity."[1]

The language of the private was not that of a mercenary. Wright of the New Jersey line frequently referred in his journal to the Philistines, meaning the enemy, and commented upon the "diabolical rage of the parliamentary tools on Bunker Hill" (then held by the British).[2] Another private, a Massachusetts man, referred to "the wicked enemy,"[3] and a less restrained writer to "the butchers belonging to the tyrant of Great Britain."[4] Private McCurtin, of Maryland, referred to General Gage during the siege of Boston as "that Crocodile and second Pharoe, namely Tom: Gage."[5] Corporal Farnsworth, a very religious man, spoke of the burning of Charlestown by "that infernal Villain Thomas Gage," and to the possession of Boston by "our Unnatteral enemyes."[6]

---

[1] Nathan Davis's History; in Historical Magazine, April, 1868, p. 205.

[2] *Ibid.*, p. 209.

[3] Military Journals of Two Private Soldiers, p. 66.

[4] D. McCurtin's Journal; in T. Balch's Papers (1857), p. 33.

[5] *Ibid.*, p. 17.

[6] A. Farnsworth's Diary; in Massachusetts Historical Society Proceedings, January, 1898, pp. 84, 88.

Plain speaking and independence of thought were characteristic of a people less bound by class distinctions and therefore less accustomed to obey than those of equal educational and property qualifications in the Old World. These traits made their impress upon events. Said Governor Trumbull: " The pulse of a New England man beats high for liberty. His engagement in the service he thinks purely voluntary—therefore in his estimation, when the time of his enlistment was out, he thinks himself not holden, without further engagement." [1] This feeling accounts for a serious reduction of the army besieging Boston in the winter of 1775–76; as company after company broke camp and marched away, the troops hissed, showing unmistakably that many disapproved of the action.[2] Personal loyalty sometimes found its expression in hand-to-hand encounters between the ardent patriots in the army and those whose zeal was open to question. A New Englander, it is said, felt no hesitation, when meeting a halfhearted Nova Scotia volunteer (popularly called a Holy Ghoster), in knocking him down on

[1] Stuart's Trumbull (1859), p. 224.

[2] Captain Nathan Hale attributed the departure of volunteers to a scarcity of provisions. In any case the men took affairs into their own hands. *Ibid.*, p. 223.

the spot without pretext or preliminary explanation.

The following picture of the private soldier, singing as he suffered, is by a surgeon at Valley Forge; he studied the details day by day, the humorous and pathetic, the light and the shade:

" See the poor Soldier, when in health—with what chearfullness he meets his foes and encounters every hardship—if barefoot—he labours thro' the Mud & Cold with a Song in his mouth extolling War & Washington [1]—if his food be bad—he eats it notwithstanding with seeming content—blesses God for a good Stomach—and whisles it into digestion. But harkee Patience—a moment—There comes a Soldier—His bare feet are seen thro' his worn Shoes—his legs nearly naked from the tatter'd remains of an only pair of stockings— his Breeches not sufficient to cover his Nakedness—his shirt hanging in Strings—his hair dishevell'd—his face meagre—his whole appearance pictures a person forsaken & discouraged. He comes, and crys with an air of wretchedness & dispair—I am Sick—my feet lame— my legs are sore—my body cover'd with this tormenting Itch—my cloaths are worn out—my Constitution is broken—my former Activity is exhausted by fatigue— hunger & Cold—I fail fast I shall soon be no more!

---

[1] Mitchel Sewall's ode, the only one mentioned, as far as I have noticed, in the diaries here cited as actually sung by the rank and file of the army.

and all the reward I shall get will be—'Poor Will is dead.' " [1]

There was another side to the war picture. Enthusiasm and excitement enabled men, bred to a city life, to endure exposure in the dead of winter that under ordinary circumstances must have proved fatal. Dr. Benjamin Rush has called attention to the apparent effect of the victory at Trenton in 1776 upon some 1,500 Philadelphia militia. During a period of five weeks or more these men, unaccustomed to hardship, slept in barns and upon the bare ground, with a record of only two cases of sickness and one of death. The plain living and comparatively regular hours of camp life are said to have saved some men from consumption and other diseases; while the change of environment from the too frequent irritation and pettiness of village life delivered nervous persons from their own misfortunes and freshened their minds.[2]

Two questions arise in connection with the men of the Revolution, How many served against Great Britain? and What became of the survivors

[1] Dr. A. Waldo's Diary ; in Historical Magazine, May, 1861, p. 131.

[2] Dr. Benjamin Rush, in Massachusetts Magazine for 1791, pp. 284, 360.

after the war had closed? General Knox, in a report to Congress, attempted to answer the first of these,[1] but his tables are hopelessly confusing, since they are based upon the number of men *to be* enlisted rather than upon the number of those who engaged themselves, and upon records of the years of their service rather than upon the number of men performing this service.[2] By the roughest kind of calculation the total number of men who served as Continentals or as militiamen during any part of the eight years of the war must have been far in excess of 232,000, the usual estimate, based upon Knox's tables. Many of these men died of wounds or disease, and many more returned to their homes broken in health and without suitable occupation. The names of officers and privates who received pensions have been recorded by the Government from time to time; mention should be made, first, of a list, giving 1,730 pensioners whose names were on the rolls June 1, 1813;[3] again, of another, giving about 16,000

[1] Knox's Report; in American State Papers, Military Affairs, vol. 1, p. 14.

[2] Explained in Justin Winsor's paper; in Massachusetts Historical Society Proceedings, January, 1886, p. 204. For an example of the misleading tables see Harper's Book of Facts (New York, 1895), under "Army," p. 47.

[3] Thirteenth Congress, First Session ; Executive reports, letter

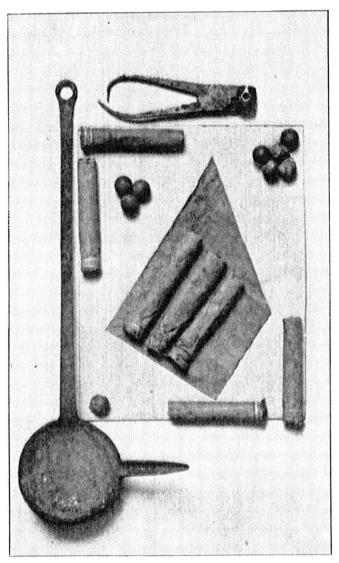

Gray cartridge paper, with cartridges and ball, found in the attic
of the church at Shirley Centre, Mass., by J. E. L. Hazen; also
bullet mould and melting pot.

names in 1820;[1] of a third, three thick volumes[2] (a report from the Secretary of War in obedience to resolves of the Senate of June 5th and 30th, 1834, and March 3, 1835); and of a fourth list, a thin volume which appeared in 1840. Portraits of several aged pensioners may be seen in E. B. Hillard's work on "The Last Men of the Revolution," and one of Ralph Farnham, called the last survivor of the battle of Bunker Hill, will be found in C. W. Clarence's biographical sketch of him. Samuel Downing, a private of the New Hampshire line, was the last surviving Revolutionary pensioner under the general acts which placed all State and national pensioners, and finally all men who had served nine months, on the rolls. He died February 18, 1869, at the age of one hundred and seven.[3] The last sur-

from Secretary of War. Reprinted in Minnesota Historical Society Collections.

[1] Sixteenth Congress, First Session, House Documents, vol. 4, No. 55. See also Twenty-first Congress, Second Session, House Documents, vol. 2, No. 31, for list of those rejected, with reasons; and vol. 3, No. 86, for an invalid pension roll.

[2] Twenty-third Congress, First Session, Senate Documents, vols. 12, 13, 14.

[3] Harper's Book of Facts (1895), pp. 621, 682. Downing's kindly face, framed in snow-white hair, serves as a frontispiece for Mr. Hillard's book.

vivor placed on the rolls by special act of Congress was Daniel F. Bakeman, of Cattaraugus County, New York, who died April 5, 1869, at the age of one hundred and nine. As late as June 30, 1899, four widows of soldiers of the war appeared on the pension rolls.[1]

In the preceding pages officers have been quoted as authorities on the rank and file. It would hardly do to quote seriously the opinions which a private at the age of one hundred and two held in regard to his superiors, but a line from Downing's observations on each of the great names of the war may, nevertheless, not be out of place :

Of Arnold : A bloody fellow he was. He didn't care for nothing; he'd ride right in. It was " Come on, boys ! " 'twasn't " Go, boys ! " . . . there wasn't any waste timber in him. He was a stern looking man but kind to his soldiers. They didn't treat him right . . . but he ought to have been true.

Of Gates : Gates was an " old granny " looking fellow.

Of Washington : Oh ! but you never got a smile out of him. He was a nice man. We loved him. They'd sell their lives for him.

[1] World Almanac, 1900, p. 165.

Alexander Milliner, another aged pensioner, said:

Of Arnold: Arnold was a smart man; they didn't sarve him quite straight.

Of Washington: He was a good man, a beautiful man. He was always pleasant; never changed countenance, but wore the same in defeat and retreat as in victory.

Pension legislation relating to the Revolution was summarized by the Commissioner in his report of October 19, 1857.[1] The first general act (March 18, 1818) was for the benefit of officers and men in need of assistance who had served in the Continental army or navy to the close of the war or for nine consecutive months, and allowed to privates $8 a month; the act of May 15, 1828, gave to privates in the Continental line who had served to the close of the war the amount of their full pay, whether in need of help or not; the act of June 7, 1832, gave to all persons who had done any military service in the Revolutionary War for six months a fourth of full pay, with increase varying according to the term of service up to two years. These acts were followed by what were known as "the widows' acts." The

[1] Appended to Secretary of Interior's Report: Thirty-fifth Congress, First Session, Senate Documents, vol. 2.

total expenditure to the year 1857 exceeded $60,-000,000, or less than one-half the *yearly* pension appropriation now made on account of later wars. To state the comparison in another way, the Civil War (the chief source of the pension roll) in forty years has cost in pensions forty times what the Revolutionary War cost in eighty years.[1] This is a commentary on the growth of the country from 1783 to 1865 in population, territory, and wealth, and perhaps also on an increasing willingness to accept public aid.

In the years immediately following the close of the war the veterans too often were obliged to depend wholly or in part upon friends or children for support; they went from town to town, telling their stories at the village inn or by the fireside to the boys and girls of that time, who have passed them on to our own day. The hardest misfortunes came in the summer of 1783. Elijah Fisher's experiences are recorded in his journal, and as he had served for several years as a private soldier they may be taken as a fair picture of the trials of the less fortunate enlisted men. He left the " old Jarsey preasen ship " April 9, 1783, and landed in New York City; that night he slept at the City Hall Tavern, where he was

[1] World Almanac for 1900, p. 164.

[246]

well treated and provided with a shirt. He continues :

" The 10th. I Leaves Mr. Franceps and so goes about the City to se it and went into Nombers of there shopes and would say your servent gentlefolks, I wish you much Joy with the nuse of peace, I hope it will be a long and a lasting one, some of them would be Very well pleased with it and would wish me the same (and others would be on the other hand) and said that their surcomstances poor at preasent but now they hoped they would be better. I said what then do you think of us poor prisners that have neither Money nor frinds and have ben long absent from our homes, then some of of them would pity us and would give us something, some half a Dollar some a quarter, some less, some nothing but frowns."

The next afternoon Fisher sailed for Boston ; he arrived in due time, and the story proceeds:

" The 14th. I Leaves Mr. Brimers at the Planes. I gos through Brookline and in to old Cambridge, from there to the Tenhills and then to Charleston, and then Cross the farray in to Boston, but there was so meny that Come from the army and from see that had no homes that would work for little or nothing but there vitels that I Could not find any Employment, so stays in Boston till the seventeenth ; in the meenwhile one Day after I had ben Inquiring and had ben on bord severel of there Vesels but could git into no bisnes neither by see nor Land,

[247]

"The 16th. I Com Down by the markett and sits Down all alone, allmost Descureged, and begun to think over how that I had ben in the army, what ill success I had met with there and all so how I was ronged by them I worked for at home, and lost all last winter, and now that I could not get into any besness and no home, which you may well think how I felt; but then Come into my mind that there ware thousands in wors sircumstances then I was, and having food and rament [I ought to] be Content, and that I had nothing to reflect on myself, and I [resolved] to do my endever and leave the avent to Provedance, and after that I felt as contented as need to be."[1]

With this quaint narrative of the troubles that fell to the lot of the Revolutionary veteran and the consolations that were his also, this record of the private soldier closes. He was a humble instrument in a great cause; he profited by an opportunity that does not come in every generation. Whether France or Washington or the patriot army contributed most to bring about the peace of Paris in 1783 is of little moment. France and Washington long ago had their due; it has been the purpose of these pages to give the private soldier under Washington whatever share in the victory was his by right of the danger, privation, and toil that he endured.

[1] Elijah Fisher's Journal, pp. 23, 24. Punctuation added.

[248]

INDEX

INDEX

[251]

[252]

Index

Disease, 177; variety of, 182

Dishonesty of officers, 135

Dogs, eaten, 84

Draft, fine imposed for refusing, 50, 62

Drinking, excessive, 228–229

Driver or snapper, 120

Dunmore, Lord, his proclamation freeing servants and slaves, 22

EARTH-WORKS. See Field-works

Enlistment, term of, 28-33; checked, 34; influences to, 39; excessive, 46, 47; those exempt, 50; short term of, 62; motives controlling, 234–235

Epithets, 222, 238

Establishment, old, 27

Exchange of prisoners, 192–193

FIELD-WORKS, 152, 233; Adams's opinion, 234

Firearms, scarcity of, 113-114; imported, 115; old-time, 119; accidents in using, 112–113

Firelock, and powder, 105 *et seq.;* weakness of firelock, 108, 111; loading, 108, 110

Firing, 122-123

Fisher, Elijah, his experiences at the close of the war, 246–248

Flag of truce fired upon, 149

Flintlock. See Firelock

Flints, 119–120; life of, 120

Food, how obtained, 89. See also Ration

Food, price of, 34-36

Foraging, 209

Foreigners as deserters, 58

Fourth of July, 165

Freneau, Philip, in a prison-ship, 188

Fudg fairyouwell my friends, 168

GANO, Rev. John, 159–161

Gantlet, 175

Gates, Horatio, as seen by a private, 244

"General," in military music, 196

George III., statue of lead, 115

Goddard, John, carries stores to Concord, 10

Grass guard, 151

Index

[257]